~ *All Time* ~

FAMILY FAVORITES™

DOWN HOME COOKIN'

PUBLICATIONS INTERNATIONAL, LTD.

Louis Weber, C.E.O.
Publications International, Ltd.
7373 N. Cicero Ave.
Lincolnwood, IL 60646

Some of the products listed in this publication may be in limited distribution.

Front cover photography by Sanders Studios, Inc., Chicago

Pictured on the front cover *(clockwise from top right):* Pickled Peaches *(page 106),* Quick Dills *(page 37),* Acorn Squash with Maple Butter *(page 34),* Corn Relish *(page 36),* Green Beans with Pine Nuts *(page 32),* Baked Country Cured Ham *(page 46),* Flaky Southern Biscuits *(page 12),* Golden Hearty Cornbread *(page 12)* and Berry Cobbler *(page 106).*

Pictured on the back cover: California Apricot-Cherry Cornmeal Cobbler *(page 122).*

ISBN: 0-7853-1173-4

Manufactured in U.S.A.

8 7 6 5 4 3 2 1

Microwave Cooking: Microwave ovens may vary in wattage. The microwave cooking times given in this publication are approximate. Use the cooking times as guidelines and check for doneness before adding more time. Consult manufacturer's instructions for suitable microwave-safe dishes.

Contents

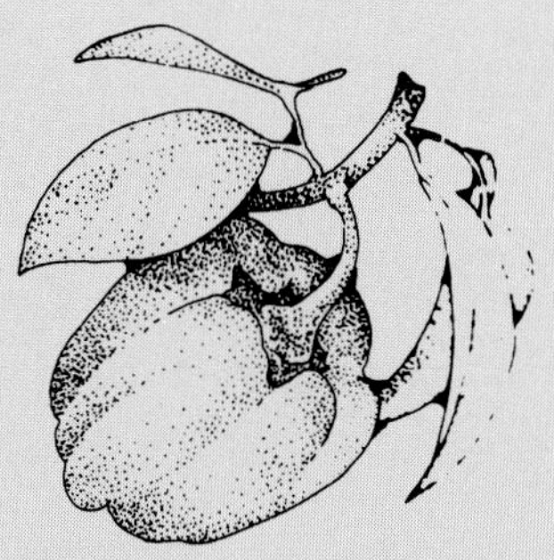

— *Hearty* —

SOUPS & BREADS

POTATO & CHEDDAR SOUP

2 cups water
2 cups peeled red potato cubes
3 tablespoons butter or margarine
1 small onion, finely chopped
3 tablespoons all-purpose flour
Red and black pepper to taste
3 cups milk
½ teaspoon sugar
1 cup shredded Cheddar cheese
1 cup cubed cooked ham

Bring water to a boil in large saucepan. Add potatoes and cook until tender. Drain, reserving liquid. Measure 1 cup, adding water if necessary. Melt butter in saucepan over medium heat. Add onion; cook and stir until tender but not brown. Add flour; season with red and black pepper. Cook 3 to 4 minutes. Gradually add potatoes, reserved liquid, milk and sugar to onion mixture; stir well. Add cheese and ham. Simmer over low heat 30 minutes, stirring frequently. *Makes 12 servings*

BACON BRUNCH BUNS

- **1 loaf (1 pound) frozen bread dough**
- **2 tablespoons (½ package) HIDDEN VALLEY RANCH® Original Ranch® with Bacon salad dressing mix**
- **¼ cup unsalted butter or margarine, melted**
- **1 cup shredded Cheddar cheese**
- **2 egg yolks**
- **1½ tablespoons cold water**
- **3 tablespoons sesame seeds**

Thaw bread dough according to package directions. Preheat oven to 375°F. On floured board, roll dough into rectangle about 18×7 inches. In small bowl, whisk together salad dressing mix and butter. Spread mixture on dough; sprinkle with cheese. Roll up tightly, jelly-roll style, pinching seam to seal. Cut into 16 slices.

Place slices cut-side down on greased jelly-roll pan. Cover with plastic wrap and let rise until doubled in bulk, about 1 hour. In small bowl, beat egg yolks and water; brush mixture over buns. Sprinkle with sesame seeds. Bake until golden brown, 25 to 30 minutes. Serve warm.

Makes 16 buns

ORANGE PECAN BREAD

- **1¾ cups all-purpose flour**
- **¾ cup sugar**
- **1 teaspoon baking powder**
- **½ teaspoon baking soda**
- **½ teaspoon salt**
- **¾ cup Florida orange juice**
- **1 egg, lightly beaten**
- **2 tablespoons butter or margarine, melted and cooled**
- **1 tablespoon grated fresh orange peel**
- **½ teaspoon almond extract**
- **½ cup chopped pitted dates**
- **½ cup chopped pecans**

Preheat oven to 350°F.

In large bowl, combine flour, sugar, baking powder, baking soda and salt. In separate bowl, combine orange juice, egg, butter, orange peel and almond extract.

Make a well in center of flour mixture and pour in orange juice mixture; stir until just combined. Stir in dates and pecans.

Pour batter into greased 9×5×3-inch loaf pan. Bake at 350°F for 50 minutes or until wooden pick inserted in center comes out clean. Cool in pan 10 minutes. Remove from pan. Cool completely on wire rack.

Makes 1 loaf

Favorite recipe from ***Florida Department of Citrus***

Bacon Brunch Buns

NAVAJO LAMB STEW WITH CORNMEAL DUMPLINGS

2 pounds lean lamb stew meat with bones, cut into 2-inch pieces *or* 1½ pounds lean boneless lamb, cut into 1½-inch cubes
1 teaspoon salt
½ teaspoon pepper
2½ tablespoons vegetable oil, divided
1 large onion, chopped
1 clove garlic, minced
4 cups water
2 tablespoons tomato paste
2 teaspoons chili powder
1 teaspoon ground coriander
3 small potatoes, cut into 1½-inch chunks
2 large carrots, cut into 1-inch pieces
1 package (10 ounces) frozen whole kernel corn
⅓ cup coarsely chopped celery leaves
Cornmeal Dumplings (recipe follows)
Whole celery leaves for garnish

Sprinkle meat with salt and pepper. Heat 2 tablespoons oil in 5-quart Dutch oven over medium-high heat. Add meat a few pieces at a time; cook until browned. Transfer meat to medium bowl. Heat remaining ½ tablespoon oil over medium heat. Add onion and garlic; cook until onion is tender. Stir in water, tomato paste, chili powder and coriander. Return meat to Dutch oven. Add potatoes, carrots, corn and chopped celery leaves. Bring to a boil. Cover; reduce heat and simmer 1 hour and 15 minutes or until meat is tender. During last 15 minutes of cooking, prepare Cornmeal Dumplings. Drop dough onto stew to make 6 dumplings. Cover and simmer 18 minutes or until dumplings are firm to the touch and wooden pick inserted in center comes out clean. To serve, spoon stew onto individual plates; serve with dumplings. Garnish with whole celery leaves.

Makes 6 servings

Cornmeal Dumplings

½ cup yellow cornmeal
½ cup all-purpose flour
1 teaspoon baking powder
¼ teaspoon salt
2½ tablespoons cold butter or margarine
½ cup milk

Combine cornmeal, flour, baking powder and salt in medium bowl. Cut in butter with fingers, pastry blender or 2 knives until mixture resembles coarse crumbs. Make a well in center; pour in milk all at once and stir with fork until mixture forms dough.

Navajo Lamb Stew with Cornmeal Dumplings

CHEDDAR CHOWDER

2 cups boiling water
2 cups caulifloweretes
1 cup diced potatoes
½ cup sliced carrots
½ cup sliced celery
¼ cup chopped onion
1½ teaspoons salt
¼ teaspoon pepper
¼ cup butter or margarine
¼ cup flour
2 cups milk
2 cups (8 ounces) SARGENTO® Classic Supreme® or Fancy Supreme® Shredded Mild or Sharp Cheddar Cheese
1 cup cubed cooked ham (optional)

In large saucepan, combine water, cauliflower, potatoes, carrots, celery, onion, salt and pepper. Bring to a boil over medium-high heat; cover and simmer 10 minutes. Do not drain. In large saucepan, melt butter. Stir in flour, then milk; heat to boiling. Continue simmering, stirring constantly, until thickened. Add Cheddar cheese; stir until melted. Add undrained vegetable mixture and ham, if desired. Heat through, but do not boil.

Makes about 8 servings

APPLE CHEDDAR MUFFINS

1 egg, slightly beaten
½ cup milk
¼ cup vegetable oil
1 cup applesauce
¼ cup sugar
1½ cups all-purpose flour
2 teaspoons baking powder
½ teaspoon salt
½ teaspoon ground cinnamon
½ cup (2 ounces) SARGENTO® Classic Supreme® Shredded Mild or Sharp Cheddar Cheese

In large bowl, combine egg, milk, oil, applesauce and sugar. Sift flour, baking powder, salt and cinnamon together; add all at once with Cheddar cheese to egg mixture. Stir only until flour mixture is moistened (batter will be lumpy). Divide batter evenly among 12 greased muffin cups. (Cups will be more than ⅔ full.) Bake at 400°F for about 20 minutes or until wooden pick inserted in center comes out clean. Let cool in muffin pan 5 minutes. Run knife around outer edges of each muffin; turn out onto rack to cool completely.

Makes 12 muffins

Left to right: Cheddar Chowder; Apple Cheddar Muffins

GOLDEN HEARTY CORNBREAD

1¼ cups cornmeal
½ cup all-purpose flour
½ teaspoon baking soda
⅛ teaspoon salt (optional)
½ cup KELLOGG'S® ALL-BRAN® cereal
¾ cup skim milk
2 egg whites, slightly beaten
3 tablespoons vegetable oil
1 cup no-salt-added whole kernel corn, drained
½ cup reduced fat Cheddar cheese
½ cup chopped green onions
Nonstick cooking spray

1. Stir together cornmeal, flour, baking soda and salt. Set aside.

2. In large mixing bowl, combine Kellogg's® All-Bran® cereal and milk. Let stand 2 minutes or until cereal is slightly softened. Add egg whites, oil, corn, cheese and onions. Add flour mixture, stirring just until combined. Spread batter into 8×8×2-inch baking pan coated with cooking spray.

3. Bake at 400°F about 40 minutes or until golden brown. Serve warm. *Makes 9 servings*

FLAKY SOUTHERN BISCUITS

2 cups all-purpose flour
1 tablespoon baking powder
½ teaspoon salt
½ cup chilled vegetable shortening
¾ cup cold milk

Preheat oven to 425°F. In large bowl, combine flour, baking powder and salt. With pastry blender, cut in shortening until mixture resembles coarse meal. Stir in milk until dough holds together. Knead gently about 1 minute. Roll dough ½ inch thick. With 2½- to 3-inch biscuit cutter, cut dough. Place 1 inch apart on ungreased cookie sheet. Bake 12 to 15 minutes or until lightly browned. *Makes 10 biscuits*

Favorite recipe from ***McIlhenny Company***

OLD-FASHIONED CARROT SOUP

1 (46-fluid ounce) can COLLEGE INN® Chicken Broth
1½ pounds carrots, cut in 1-inch pieces
4 large onions, coarsely chopped
3 stalks celery, cut in 1-inch pieces
¼ cup chopped parsley
¼ cup BLUE BONNET® 75% Vegetable Oil Spread
¼ cup all-purpose flour
2 cups milk*

*For thinner soup, add additional milk until desired consistency.

In large heavy pot, over medium-high heat, bring broth, carrots, onions, celery and parsley to a boil. Cover; reduce heat and simmer until vegetables are tender, about 30 minutes. Cool slightly. In blender container or food processor, blend mixture in batches until smooth; set aside.

In same saucepan, melt spread; blend in flour. Stir in carrot mixture and milk. Cook, stirring occasionally, until heated through. Garnish with additional parsley if desired. *Makes 8 servings*

QUICK & EASY CHILI

1½ pounds ground beef
1 large onion, chopped
1 clove garlic, minced
2 (16-ounce) cans kidney beans, drained
2 (12-ounce) jars ORTEGA® Mild or Medium Thick and Chunky Salsa
2 teaspoons chili powder
½ teaspoon dried oregano leaves
½ teaspoon ground cumin
Shredded Cheddar cheese (optional)

In 4-quart saucepan, over medium heat, cook beef, onion and garlic until beef is no longer pink, stirring occasionally to break up meat; drain. Add beans, salsa, chili powder, oregano and cumin. Cover; simmer for 30 minutes, stirring occasionally. Serve topped with cheese if desired.
Makes 6 servings

CORNSTICKS

⅔ cup yellow or blue cornmeal
⅓ cup all-purpose flour
3 tablespoons sugar
1½ teaspoons baking powder
½ teaspoon LAWRY'S® Seasoned Salt
1 cup milk
2 tablespoons butter or IMPERIAL® margarine, melted
1 egg, well beaten
2 tablespoons diced green chiles

Preheat oven to 425°F. In medium bowl, combine cornmeal, flour, sugar, baking powder and Seasoned Salt. In 4-cup measure, combine milk, butter and egg; blend well. Slowly pour into flour mixture, stirring until well blended. Stir in green chiles. Spoon batter into lightly greased corn-shaped molds. Bake on lowest rack in 425°F oven 20 to 25 minutes or until golden brown. Serve warm with whipped butter. *Makes 12 cornsticks*

TIP: For a wonderful flavor variation, try adding ¼ cup grated Cheddar cheese. If cornstick molds are not available, use an 8-inch square baking pan. Spoon batter into lightly greased pan and bake as directed.

CREAMY SHELL SOUP

- 4 cups water
- 3 to 4 chicken pieces
- 1 cup diced onions
- ¼ cup chopped celery
- ¼ cup minced parsley *or* 1 tablespoon dried parsley flakes
- 1 bay leaf
- 1 teaspoon salt
- ¼ teaspoon white pepper
- 2 medium potatoes, diced
- 4 to 5 green onions, chopped
- 3 chicken bouillon cubes
- ½ teaspoon seasoned salt
- ½ teaspoon poultry seasoning
- 4 cups milk
- 2 cups medium shell macaroni, cooked and drained
- ¼ cup butter or margarine
- ¼ cup all-purpose flour
- Ground nutmeg
- Chopped fresh parsley

Simmer water, chicken, diced onions, celery, minced parsley, bay leaf, salt and pepper in Dutch oven until chicken is tender. Remove bay leaf; discard. Remove chicken; cool. Skin, debone and cut into small cubes; set aside.

Add potatoes, green onions, bouillon cubes, seasoned salt and poultry seasoning to broth. Simmer 15 minutes. Add milk, macaroni and chicken; return to simmer.

Melt butter in skillet over medium heat. Add flour, stirring constantly, until mixture begins to brown. Add to soup; blend well. Let soup simmer on very low heat 20 minutes to blend flavors. Season to taste. Garnish with nutmeg and chopped parsley.

Makes 8 servings

Favorite recipe from **North Dakota Wheat Commission**

PINTO-SAUSAGE STEW

- ½ pound Polish sausage, cut into ¼-inch slices
- 2 cans (15 ounces each) pinto beans, undrained
- 2 medium onions, chopped (about 1½ cups)
- 1 cup tomato juice
- ½ cup PACE® Picante Sauce
- 1 medium green pepper, cut into ¾-inch pieces
- 1 teaspoon chili powder
- ½ teaspoon ground cumin
- ½ teaspoon dried oregano leaves, crushed
- ¼ cup chopped fresh cilantro

In large saucepan, combine sausage, beans with liquid, onions, tomato juice, picante sauce, green pepper, chili powder, cumin and oregano; bring to a boil. Cover and simmer 20 minutes. Top with cilantro and serve with additional picante sauce.

Makes 6 servings (about 6 cups)

Creamy Shell Soup

STREUSEL LEMON BREAD

½ cup finely chopped nuts
¼ cup firmly packed light brown sugar
½ teaspoon ground nutmeg
2 cups unsifted flour
1 teaspoon baking powder
½ teaspoon baking soda
1¼ cups granulated sugar
½ cup margarine or butter, softened
3 eggs
½ cup REALEMON® Lemon Juice from Concentrate
½ cup BORDEN® or MEADOW GOLD® Milk

Preheat oven to 350°F. In small bowl, combine nuts, brown sugar and nutmeg; set aside. Stir together flour, baking powder and baking soda; set aside. In large mixer bowl, beat granulated sugar and margarine until fluffy. Add eggs, 1 at a time, beating well after each addition. Gradually beat in ReaLemon® brand. Add milk alternately with flour mixture; stir well. Spoon half of batter into greased and floured 9×5-inch loaf pan. Sprinkle half of nut mixture over batter; top with remaining batter, spreading to pan edge. Top with remaining nut mixture. Bake 50 to 55 minutes or until wooden pick inserted near center comes out clean. Cool 15 minutes; remove from pan. Cool completely. Store tightly wrapped. *Makes one 9×5-inch loaf*

SAVORY APPLE BREAD

1 tablespoon butter or margarine
1 Golden Delicious apple, peeled, cored and diced
½ cup chopped onion
1 (16-ounce) package hot roll mix
1 cup shredded Cheddar cheese
2 tablespoons chopped sweet red pepper
1 tablespoon caraway seeds
1 cup hot (not boiling) water
1 egg, beaten

In small skillet, heat butter. Add apple and onion; cook and stir until both are tender. Set aside. In large bowl, combine hot roll mix, cheese, red pepper and caraway seeds. Stir in water, egg and reserved apple mixture; stir until dough pulls away from side of bowl.

Turn dough out onto lightly floured surface; knead 5 minutes. Cover dough with mixing bowl and let rest 5 minutes.

Grease 1½-quart round baking dish; place dough in dish. Score an "X" on top of dough with sharp knife. Cover dough and let rise 30 minutes.

When dough has risen, heat oven to 375°F; bake bread 35 minutes or until golden and hollow-sounding when gently tapped. Cool on wire rack.
Makes 8 servings

Favorite recipe from ***Washington Apple Commission***

Streusel Lemon Bread

MINESTRONE SOUP

½ cup finely chopped leeks
3 tablespoons finely chopped onion
1 clove garlic, finely chopped
2 tablespoons vegetable oil
1½ cups chopped zucchini
1½ cups chopped carrots
1½ cups chopped potatoes
½ cup thinly sliced celery
1 can (28 ounces) whole tomatoes, chopped and undrained
5 cups chicken broth
1 can (16 ounces) Great Northern beans
½ teaspoon salt
½ teaspoon dried basil leaves
¼ teaspoon black pepper
1 bay leaf
2 sprigs fresh parsley
1 package (10 ounces) frozen peas
1 cup KELLOGG'S® ALL-BRAN® cereal
3 tablespoons grated Parmesan cheese
Snipped fresh parsley

In 8-quart saucepan, cook and stir leeks, onion and garlic in oil. Add zucchini, carrots, potatoes and celery. Cook for 5 minutes, stirring frequently. Add tomatoes with liquid, broth, beans and seasonings. Cover; bring to a boil. Simmer 20 minutes; stir occasionally. Add peas; simmer 10 minutes or until tender.

Remove bay leaf and parsley. Stir in Kellogg's® All-Bran® cereal. Serve hot garnished with Parmesan cheese and snipped fresh parsley.

Makes 9 servings (1½ cups each)

BAYOU JAMBALAYA

1 medium onion, sliced
½ cup chopped green bell pepper
1 clove garlic, minced
1 cup uncooked white rice
2 tablespoons vegetable oil
1 cup water
¾ cup HEINZ® Tomato Ketchup
1 tablespoon HEINZ® Vinegar
⅛ teaspoon black pepper
⅛ teaspoon ground red pepper
1 cup cubed cooked ham
1 medium tomato, coarsely chopped
½ pound raw medium shrimp, shelled, deveined

In large skillet, cook and stir onion, green pepper, garlic and rice in oil until onion is tender. Stir in water, ketchup, vinegar, black pepper, red pepper, ham and tomato. Cover; simmer 20 to 25 minutes or until rice is tender. Add shrimp; simmer, uncovered, 3 to 5 minutes or until shrimp turn pink, stirring occasionally.

Makes 4 to 6 servings (about 6 cups)

Bayou Jambalaya

Classic Banana Bread

- 2 extra-ripe, medium DOLE® Bananas, peeled
- ¾ cup brown sugar, packed
- ½ cup margarine, softened
- 1 egg
- ¼ cup dairy sour cream
- 1 teaspoon vanilla extract
- 2¼ cups all-purpose flour
- 1 teaspoon baking powder
- ½ teaspoon baking soda
- ½ teaspoon salt
- ½ teaspoon ground cinnamon
- 1 cup DOLE® Chopped Almonds

• Preheat oven to 350°F.

• Process bananas in blender; measure 1 cup.

• Beat sugar and margarine until light and fluffy. Beat in egg. Beat in processed bananas, sour cream and vanilla until blended.

• Combine flour, baking powder, baking soda, salt and cinnamon. Stir into banana mixture. Stir in almonds.

• Pour into greased 9×5-inch loaf pan. Bake in preheated oven 65 to 70 minutes or until wooden pick inserted in center comes out clean. Cool in pan 10 minutes. Invert onto wire rack to cool completely.

Makes 1 loaf

Poppy Seed Bread

- 1 cup sugar
- ½ cup margarine, softened
- 2 eggs
- 1 teaspoon grated lemon peel
- 2 extra-ripe, medium DOLE® Bananas, peeled
- 2 cups all-purpose flour
- 2 teaspoons baking powder
- ½ teaspoon salt
- ¼ teaspoon ground cinnamon
- ¼ cup poppy seeds

• Preheat oven to 350°F.

• In large bowl, beat sugar and margarine until light and fluffy. Beat in eggs and lemon peel. Process bananas in blender; measure 1 cup.

• In small bowl, combine flour, baking powder, salt and cinnamon. Add flour mixture to egg mixture alternately with processed bananas, ending with flour mixture. Stir in poppy seeds. Spoon into greased 9×5-inch loaf pan.

• Bake in preheated oven 60 to 70 minutes or until wooden pick inserted in center comes out clean. Cool slightly in pan. Invert onto wire rack to cool completely.

Makes 1 loaf

Classic Banana Bread

CHUNKY BEEF CHILI

- 2 tablespoons vegetable oil
- 2½ pounds boneless beef chuck, cut into ½-inch pieces
- 1 cup coarsely chopped onion
- 1 cup chopped green bell pepper
- 2 cloves garlic, minced
- 1 teaspoon salt
- 1 can (28 ounces) Italian-style plum tomatoes, broken up and undrained
- 1 cup water
- 1 can (6 ounces) tomato paste
- 3 tablespoons chili powder
- 1 teaspoon dried oregano leaves
- ¼ to ½ teaspoon crushed red pepper
- 1 can (15½ ounces) red kidney beans, drained
- 6 tablespoons shredded sharp Cheddar cheese
- 6 tablespoons chopped onion

Heat oil in large skillet or Dutch oven over medium-high heat. Add boneless beef chuck pieces, 1 cup chopped onion, green pepper and garlic; cook until beef is evenly browned. Pour off drippings. Sprinkle salt over beef. Add tomatoes with juice, water, tomato paste, chili powder, oregano and crushed red pepper. Cover tightly; reduce heat and simmer 1½ hours or until beef is tender. Add beans; continue cooking, uncovered, 20 to 30 minutes. Serve with cheese and additional chopped onion. *Makes 8 servings*

Favorite recipe from ***National Live Stock & Meat Board***

CANDY WAGNER'S TEX-MEX STEW

- 2 pounds ground beef
- 2 large garlic cloves, minced
- 3 tablespoons vegetable oil
- 1 can (28 ounces) whole tomatoes
- 1 cup PACE® Picante Sauce
- 1 teaspoon ground cumin
- Salt and pepper to taste
- 1 can (17 ounces) whole kernel corn, drained
- 1 can (15 ounces) pinto beans, drained
- 8 green onions with tops, sliced (about 1½ cups)
- Chopped fresh cilantro (optional)

Brown meat with garlic in oil in Dutch oven; drain meat. Drain and coarsely chop tomatoes, reserving juice. Add tomatoes, reserved juice, picante sauce, cumin, salt and pepper to meat mixture. Bring to a boil; reduce heat. Cover and simmer 20 to 30 minutes. Add corn, beans and onions; continue cooking, uncovered, 10 minutes. Top with cilantro, if desired, and serve with additional picante sauce.

Makes 6 to 8 servings (about 10 cups)

Chunky Beef Chili

VEGETABLE DISHES

FRESH VEGETABLE CASSEROLE

8 small new potatoes
8 baby carrots
1 small cauliflower, broken into florets
4 stalks asparagus, cut into 1-inch pieces
3 tablespoons butter or margarine
3 tablespoons all-purpose flour
2 cups milk
Salt
Pepper
¾ cup (3 ounces) shredded Cheddar cheese
Chopped fresh cilantro

Cook vegetables until crisp-tender. Arrange vegetables in buttered 2-quart casserole. To make sauce, melt butter in medium saucepan over medium heat. Stir in flour until smooth. Gradually stir in milk. Cook until thickened, stirring constantly. Season to taste with salt and pepper. Add cheese, stirring until cheese is melted. Pour sauce over vegetables and sprinkle with cilantro. Bake in preheated 350°F oven 15 minutes or until heated through. *Makes 4 to 6 servings*

CREAMY CORN AU GRATIN

½ cup green onion slices
½ cup chopped red pepper
¼ cup PARKAY® Margarine, divided
2 (10-ounce) packages sweet corn, thawed, drained
½ pound VELVEETA® Pasteurized Process Cheese Spread, cubed
⅔ cup crushed tortilla chips
½ teaspoon Mexican seasoning
2 tablespoons chopped cilantro

- Cook and stir onions and pepper in 2 tablespoons margarine. Reduce heat to low.
- Stir in corn and process cheese spread. Cook 5 to 7 minutes or until process cheese spread is melted and mixture is thoroughly heated, stirring occasionally.
- Melt remaining margarine in separate pan; stir in tortilla chips and seasoning. Cook over medium heat 3 minutes; stir in cilantro.
- Spoon corn mixture into serving bowl; sprinkle with tortilla mixture. Garnish with additional cilantro and red pepper. *Makes 6 servings*

Preparation Time: 25 minutes

MICROWAVE DIRECTIONS: Microwave onions, peppers and 2 tablespoons margarine in 1½-quart microwavable bowl on HIGH 2 to 3 minutes or until vegetables are tender. Stir in corn and process cheese spread. Microwave 5 to 7 minutes or until process cheese spread is melted and mixture is thoroughly heated, stirring every 3 minutes. Microwave remaining margarine in 1-quart microwavable bowl 1 minute. Stir in tortilla chips and seasoning. Microwave 2 minutes, stirring after 1 minute; stir in cilantro. Continue as directed.

Microwave Cooking Time: 13 minutes

VARIATION: Substitute ¼ teaspoon ground cumin and ¼ teaspoon chili powder for Mexican seasoning.

COUNTRY-STYLE POTATO SALAD

2 pounds cooked red potatoes, peeled and diced
3 green onions, cut into ½-inch pieces
10 cherry tomatoes, halved
2 hard-cooked eggs, chopped
⅓ cup mayonnaise
⅓ cup GREY POUPON® Dijon or Country Dijon Mustard
2 tablespoons red wine vinegar
½ teaspoon garlic powder
⅛ teaspoon ground black pepper

In large bowl, combine potatoes, green onions, tomatoes and eggs; set aside.

In small bowl, blend remaining ingredients; stir into potato mixture, tossing to coat well. Cover; chill at least 2 hours to blend flavors.

Makes 6 (1¼-cup) servings

Creamy Corn au Gratin

SPINACH BAKE

2 eggs, beaten
¾ cup MIRACLE WHIP® Salad Dressing, divided
2 (10-ounce) packages frozen chopped spinach, thawed, well drained
1 (14-ounce) can artichoke hearts, drained, cut into quarters
½ cup sour cream
¼ cup (1 ounce) KRAFT® 100% Grated Parmesan Cheese
6 crisply cooked bacon slices, crumbled

• Combine eggs and ½ cup salad dressing, mixing until well blended. Add spinach and artichokes; mix lightly. Spoon mixture into lightly greased 10×6-inch baking dish. Combine remaining salad dressing, sour cream and cheese; mix well. Spoon over spinach mixture. Bake at 350°F 30 minutes or until set. Sprinkle with bacon.

Makes 8 servings

Prep Time: 10 minutes
Bake Time: 30 minutes

MICROWAVE DIRECTIONS: Substitute 1½-quart microwavable casserole for 10×6-inch baking dish. Combine eggs and ½ cup salad dressing in casserole, mixing until well blended. Add spinach and artichokes; mix lightly. Microwave on HIGH (100% power) 8 to 9 minutes or until thoroughly heated, stirring every 3 minutes. Combine remaining salad dressing, sour cream and cheese; mix well. Spoon over spinach mixture. Microwave on HIGH (100% power) 1½ to 2 minutes or until sour cream mixture is warmed. (*Do not overcook.*) Sprinkle with bacon. Let stand 5 minutes.

MICROWAVE TIP: To thaw spinach, place frozen spinach in 1½-quart microwavable casserole; cover. Microwave on HIGH (100% power) 5 minutes. Break apart with fork; drain well.

CAJUN-STYLE GREEN BEANS

2 pounds green beans, trimmed
½ cup diced salt pork
1 clove garlic, minced
2 tablespoons white wine vinegar
1 tablespoon Dijon-style mustard
1 teaspoon sugar
½ teaspoon TABASCO® pepper sauce
¼ cup chopped celery leaves

In medium saucepan, in 1 inch boiling salted water, cook beans covered 10 minutes or until crisp-tender. Drain. In small skillet over medium-high heat, cook salt pork 2 to 3 minutes to render fat. Reduce heat; add garlic and cook 1 minute. Stir in vinegar, mustard, sugar and TABASCO sauce. Remove from heat; stir in celery leaves. Toss with beans to coat.

Makes 8 servings

AKED MASHED

TON® Recipe Secrets®
Soup Mix
shed potatoes*
l Cheddar or Swiss cheese
nces), divided
green onions (optional)
beaten
VRY'S® Seasoned Pepper

ot use salt when preparing hot mashed potatoes.

MICROWAVE DIRECTIONS: In lightly greased 1½-quart microwavable casserole, thoroughly combine all ingredients except ¼ cup cheese. Microwave, covered, at HIGH (100% power), turning casserole occasionally, 7 minutes or until heated through. Top with remaining cheese, then let stand covered 5 minutes.

Makes about 8 servings

CONVENTIONAL DIRECTIONS: Preheat oven to 375°F. In lightly greased 1½-quart casserole, thoroughly combine all ingredients except ¼ cup cheese. Bake 40 minutes. Top with remaining cheese and bake an additional 5 minutes or until cheese is melted.

OKRA-BACON CASSEROLE

1½ pounds young fresh okra
3 large tomatoes, chopped
1 medium onion, chopped
1 small green pepper, chopped
½ teaspoon TABASCO® pepper sauce
5 slices bacon

Preheat oven to 350°F. Slice okra into thin rounds. In greased 2½-quart casserole, arrange okra, tomatoes, onion and green pepper. Season with TABASCO sauce. Place bacon on top. Bake uncovered 1½ hours or until okra is tender.

Makes 6 to 8 servings

NOTE: Two (10-ounce) packages frozen okra, thawed, may be substituted for fresh okra. Bake casserole 1 hour.

MICROWAVE DIRECTIONS: In 2½-quart microwavable casserole place bacon; cover with paper towel. Cook on HIGH (100% power) 4 to 5 minutes or until crisp; remove to paper towel to cool, then crumble and set aside. Into drippings in same casserole place okra, onion and green pepper; season with TABASCO sauce. Cover loosely with plastic wrap; cook on HIGH (100% power) 15 to 18 minutes or until okra is just tender. Add tomatoes. Cover; cook on HIGH (100% power) 1 to 2 minutes or until tomatoes are tender. Sprinkle with reserved bacon before serving.

CARROTS SAUCILY SPICED

1 pound carrots, cut into ½-inch diagonal slices
¼ cup HEINZ® Tomato Ketchup
1½ tablespoons light brown sugar
1 tablespoon butter or margarine
⅛ teaspoon ground allspice

In medium saucepan, cook carrots in boiling water to cover until crisp-tender; drain. In medium skillet or saucepan, combine ketchup, brown sugar, butter and allspice; heat through. Add carrots; turn and baste with sauce until heated through.

Makes 4 to 6 servings (about 2½ cups)

ROSEMARY GARLIC POTATOES

4 large red skin potatoes, cut into wedges (about 2 pounds)
1½ teaspoons dried rosemary leaves
1 teaspoon garlic powder
2 tablespoons FLEISCHMANN'S® Margarine, melted

In large bowl, toss potatoes with rosemary and garlic. On lightly greased baking pan, arrange potatoes in single layer; drizzle with margarine. Broil 4 inches from heat source for 25 to 30 minutes or until tender, turning potatoes over once.

Makes 4 servings

RED CABBAGE 'N' APPLES

¼ cup margarine or butter
⅓ cup REALEMON® Lemon Juice from Concentrate
¼ cup firmly packed light brown sugar
¼ cup water
½ teaspoon caraway seeds
½ teaspoon salt
4 cups shredded red cabbage
2 medium all-purpose apples, cored and coarsely chopped

In large saucepan, melt margarine; stir in ReaLemon® brand, sugar, water, caraway and salt. Add cabbage and apples; bring to a boil. Reduce heat; cover and simmer 25 to 30 minutes.

Makes 6 to 8 servings

MICROWAVE DIRECTIONS: In 2-quart round microwavable dish, melt margarine on HIGH (100% power) 45 seconds. Stir in ReaLemon® brand, sugar, water, caraway and salt; add cabbage and apples. Cook covered on HIGH (100% power) 15 to 20 minutes, stirring every 5 minutes. Let stand 2 minutes before serving.

Carrots Saucily Spiced

GREEN BEANS WITH PINE NUTS

- **1 pound green beans, ends removed**
- **2 tablespoons butter or margarine**
- **2 tablespoons pine nuts**
- **Salt**
- **Pepper**

Cook beans in 1 inch water in covered 3-quart saucepan 4 to 8 minutes or until crisp-tender; drain. Melt butter in large skillet over medium heat. Add pine nuts; cook, stirring frequently, until golden. Add beans; stir gently to coat beans with butter. Season with salt and pepper to taste.

Makes 4 servings

FRESH CORN WITH ADOBE BUTTER

- **½ teaspoon chili powder**
- **1 teaspoon lime juice**
- **¼ cup butter or margarine, softened**
- **Salt**
- **4 ears yellow or white corn, husks and silk removed**

Moisten chili powder with lime juice in small bowl. Add butter; stir until well blended. Season to taste with salt. Place in small crock or bowl. Place corn in 5-quart pan; cover with cold water. Cover; bring to a boil. Boil 1 minute. Turn off heat; let stand 2 minutes or until corn is tender. Drain. Serve with butter mixture.

Makes 4 servings

GLAZED SWEET POTATOES AND TURNIPS

- **4 medium sweet potatoes, peeled, cut in chunks**
- **4 medium turnips, peeled, cut in chunks**
- **1 cup Florida orange juice**
- **⅓ cup brown sugar**
- **¼ cup butter or margarine, melted**
- **½ teaspoon mace**
- **½ teaspoon salt**
- **2 Florida oranges, peeled, sliced**

In large saucepan in 1 inch boiling water, cook potatoes and turnips until crisp-tender, about 30 minutes.

Preheat oven to 400°F.

Place vegetables in 2-quart shallow baking dish. In small bowl, combine orange juice, sugar, butter, mace and salt. Pour over vegetables.

Bake, uncovered, in 400°F oven about 30 minutes. Baste often with pan juices. Vegetables are done when pan juices are reduced and vegetables are glazed. Garnish with orange slices.

Makes 8 servings

Favorite recipe from ***Florida Department of Citrus***

Top to bottom: Green Beans with Pine Nuts; Fresh Corn with Adobe Butter

ACORN SQUASH WITH MAPLE BUTTER

2 medium acorn squash*
LAWRY'S® Seasoned Salt
3 tablespoons IMPERIAL® Margarine or butter
3 tablespoons MRS. BUTTERWORTH'S® Maple Syrup
¼ teaspoon ground nutmeg (optional)

*Butternut squash can be substituted for acorn squash.

Pierce squash with fork. Bake in 375°F oven 1 to 1½ hours or until fork-tender. Cut squash in half crosswise. Slice off ends, if necessary, so halves will be level. Remove seeds. Sprinkle squash with Seasoned Salt. In baking dish, place squash cut-side up. Divide margarine and syrup among halves. Bake 5 minutes. Sprinkle with Seasoned Salt and nutmeg. *Makes 4 servings*

PRESENTATION: Serve in quarters or sliced ½ inch thick.

MICROWAVE DIRECTIONS: Pierce squash in several places; microwave whole squash on HIGH (100% power) 10 to 12 minutes or until fork-tender; let stand 2 minutes and cut in half crosswise. Slice off ends, if necessary, so halves will be level. Remove seeds. Sprinkle squash with Seasoned Salt. In 13×9×2-inch microwavable baking dish, place squash cut-side up. Divide margarine and maple syrup among halves. Cover with plastic wrap, venting one corner. Microwave on HIGH (100% power) 30 seconds; brush syrup mixture over cut surface and microwave on HIGH (100% power) 30 seconds longer. Sprinkle with Seasoned Salt and nutmeg; let squash stand 3 minutes before serving.

CHEDDAR BROCCOLI CORN BAKE

¼ cup margarine, divided
2 tablespoons all-purpose flour
¼ teaspoon salt
1½ cups skim milk
1½ cups (6 ounces) shredded Cheddar cheese
2 cups KELLOGG'S® CORN FLAKES® cereal, crushed, divided
1 can (16 ounces) corn, drained
2 packages (10 ounces each) frozen broccoli spears, cooked and drained

1. Melt 2 tablespoons margarine in large saucepan over low heat. Stir in flour and salt. Add milk gradually, stirring until smooth. Increase heat to medium and cook until bubbly and thickened, stirring constantly. Add cheese, stirring until melted. Stir in ¼ cup crushed Kellogg's® Corn Flakes® cereal and corn and remove from heat.

2. Arrange broccoli in 12×7½×2-inch (2-quart) glass baking dish. Pour cheese sauce over broccoli.

3. Melt remaining margarine in saucepan; stir in remaining cereal. Sprinkle over casserole. Bake at 350°F 30 minutes or until heated. *Makes 7 cups*

Acorn Squash with Maple Butter

CLOCK
LOW
M-LOW
DEFROST
MED
M-HIGH
HIGH
STOP
CLEAR
START

CORN RELISH

16 to 20 medium-size ears fresh corn in husks (about 10 cups fresh whole kernel corn)
1½ cups chopped green bell peppers
1½ cups chopped red bell peppers
1 cup chopped celery
1 cup chopped onions
4 cups white vinegar (labeled 5% acidity)
2¼ cups sugar
1 cup water
2 tablespoons mustard seed
1 tablespoon plus 1 teaspoon KERR® Pickling Salt
1 teaspoon celery seed
½ teaspoon ground turmeric

Husk corn; remove silk and wash. Drop in boiling water. Return to a boil; boil 5 minutes. Immediately dip in cold water. Cut kernels from cobs. (Do not scrape cobs.) Measure 10 cups cut corn. Combine corn, peppers, celery, onions, vinegar, sugar, water, mustard seed, pickling salt, celery seed and turmeric in 8-quart saucepan. Bring to a boil over medium-high heat; boil 15 minutes, stirring occasionally.

Immediately fill hot pint jars with corn mixture, leaving ½-inch headspace. Carefully run nonmetal spatula down inside of jars to remove trapped air bubbles. Wipe jar tops and threads clean. Place hot lids on jars; screw bands on firmly. Process in Boiling Water Canner (directions follow) 15 minutes.

Makes 6 to 7 pints

Boiling Water Canner Directions: Examine jar tops. Tops with defects will prevent jar from sealing. Wash jars and keep hot to prevent breakage when filled with hot food and placed in canner for processing. Jars to be processed in Boiling Water Canner for less than 10 minutes need to be sterilized. To sterilize, cover jars with water; boil for 10 minutes. Leave in hot water until ready to use.

Examine screwbands. Use only those free from rust and dents. Examine lids. Use only those free from dents and scratches, with a complete ring of sealing compound in the groove. Wash lids; pour boiling water over lids and leave them in hot water for at least 3 minutes or until ready to use. Do not boil or reuse lids.

Fill hot jars as directed, leaving appropriate headspace. Prepare only enough jars of food at one time to fill canner. Place hot lids on jars with sealing compound next to jar top. Center on jars. Screw bands on firmly.

Partially fill canner with water; bring to a simmer. Using jar lifter, place jars, without tipping, onto rack in canner. Increase heat to high; bring to a boil. Cover; reduce heat slightly to maintain gentle, steady boil. Begin timing. Be sure water stays boiling and that it covers jars by 2 inches, adding more boiling water if needed.

When proper time is reached, turn off heat. Remove jars with jar lifter, making sure food does not touch lid. Place on rack or dry towel at least 1 inch apart, free from drafts. Cool overnight. Do not cover while cooling. Do not retighten screwbands after processing.

QUICK DILLS

6 pounds 3- to 5-inch pickling cucumbers
6 cups water
3 cups white vinegar (labeled 5% acidity)
½ cup KERR® Pickling Salt
12 to 24 heads fresh dill
6 to 12 cloves garlic (optional)

Wash cucumbers and remove 1/16 inch from blossom end. Soak in ice water for 24 hours. Drain. Combine water, vinegar and pickling salt in 6-quart saucepan. Bring to a boil over high heat. Meanwhile, place 1 to 2 heads of dill and 1 to 2 cloves garlic in hot quart jars. Firmly pack cucumbers into jars, leaving ½-inch headspace. Top with additional 1 to 2 heads of dill. Immediately fill jars with hot vinegar mixture, leaving ½-inch headspace. Carefully run nonmetal spatula down inside of jars to remove trapped air bubbles. Wipe jar tops and threads clean. Place lids on hot jars and screw bands on firmly. Process in Boiling Water Canner (page 36) for 15 minutes. For best flavor, let stand 2 to 3 weeks in jars before serving.

Makes 6 quarts

WONDERFULLY FLAVORED SKILLET GREENS

4 tablespoons margarine
2 cups chopped onions
2 tablespoons Chef Paul Prudhomme's SEAFOOD MAGIC®, in all
½ pound smoked (preferably not water-cured) picnic ham or lean smoked ham, cut into ½-inch pieces
2 cups peeled, chopped tomatoes
1 teaspoon minced garlic
2 bay leaves
1¼ pounds cleaned and picked over mustard and/or collard greens, torn into pieces (about 12 packed cups)
2 cups water, in all

Melt margarine in 4-quart saucepan over high heat. Add onions and sauté about 4 minutes, stirring occasionally. Add 1 tablespoon of the Seafood Magic®, stirring well. Cook until onions start to brown, about 3 minutes, stirring occasionally. Add ham and cook about 2 minutes, stirring fairly often. Add tomatoes, garlic and bay leaves, stirring well; cook about 1 minute. Add greens and cook about 7 minutes, stirring occasionally. Stir in remaining Seafood Magic® and cook about 2 minutes. Add ½ cup water; reduce heat to low and simmer about 20 minutes, stirring occasionally. Add remaining water and continue simmering until greens are tender and flavors blend, about 25 minutes more, stirring occasionally. Discard bay leaves and serve immediately.

Makes 6 servings

BAKED POTATO SPEARS

3 large baking potatoes
¼ cup MIRACLE WHIP® Light Reduced Calorie Salad Dressing
Onion salt
Pepper
Parma Dip (recipe follows)
Hearty Barbecue Dip (recipe follows)

- Cut potatoes lengthwise into wedges. Brush with salad dressing. Season with onion salt and pepper.
- Place on greased 15×10×1-inch jelly roll pan.
- Bake at 375°F, 50 minutes or until tender and golden brown.
- Prepare Parma Dip and Hearty Barbecue Dip. Serve with potatoes. *Makes 4 servings*

Parma Dip

1 cup MIRACLE WHIP® Light Reduced Calorie Salad Dressing
¼ cup (1 ounce) KRAFT® 100% Grated Parmesan Cheese
¼ cup milk
1 tablespoon chopped chives

- Combine ingredients; mix well. *Makes 1¼ cups*

Hearty Barbecue Dip

½ cup MIRACLE WHIP® Light Reduced Calorie Salad Dressing
¼ cup KRAFT® Thick 'n Spicy Barbecue Sauce with Honey
2 tablespoons chopped onion
2 tablespoons chopped green pepper

- Combine ingredients; mix well. *Makes 1 cup*

Preparation Time: 10 minutes
Baking Time: 50 minutes

TIP: For a more blended flavor, prepare dips ahead of time. Cover; chill.

OLD-FASHIONED COLE SLAW

½ cup reduced calorie mayonnaise
2 tablespoons milk
1 tablespoon white vinegar
½ teaspoon sugar
Salt and pepper to taste
1 bag (1 pound) DOLE® Cole Slaw Blend

- Combine mayonnaise, milk, vinegar, sugar, salt and pepper in glass measure.
- Place Cole Slaw Blend in large bowl. Pour dressing over mixture. Toss to coat with dressing.
- Cover; refrigerate at least 1 hour for flavors to blend. *Makes 8 servings*

Baked Potato Spears

CORN PUDDING SOUFFLÉ

2 tablespoons butter or margarine
2 tablespoons all-purpose flour
Half-and-half
1 can (17 ounces) whole kernel corn, drained, liquid reserved
¼ cup canned chopped green chilies, drained
Dash garlic powder
2 eggs, separated
¼ cup cream-style cottage cheese

Melt butter in medium saucepan over medium heat. Stir in flour until smooth. Add enough half-and-half to corn liquid to measure 1 cup. Gradually stir liquid into saucepan. Continue stirring until sauce is smooth and hot. Stir in corn, chilies and garlic powder.

Bring to a boil over medium heat, stirring constantly. Reduce heat to low. Beat egg yolks in small bowl. Stir about ¼ cup of the hot sauce into egg yolks, beating constantly. Stir egg yolk mixture back into sauce. Remove from heat; stir in cottage cheese. Beat egg whites in narrow bowl until stiff peaks form. Fold egg whites into corn mixture. Pour into ungreased 1½-quart soufflé dish. Bake in preheated 350°F oven 30 minutes or until wooden pick inserted in center comes out clean.

Makes 4 to 6 servings

TOMATO GINGER APPLE SALAD

2 Golden Delicious or Granny Smith apples, cored and sliced into ¼-inch rings
4 medium tomatoes, sliced into ¼-inch rings
¼ cup thinly sliced radishes
¼ cup chopped parsley
¼ cup vegetable oil
2 teaspoons grated fresh ginger
1 teaspoon sugar
1 teaspoon lemon juice
½ teaspoon grated lemon peel
Salt and pepper to taste
Parsley or cilantro sprigs (optional)

Arrange apple and tomato slices alternately on serving platter; sprinkle with radishes and parsley. In small bowl, combine oil, ginger, sugar, lemon juice and lemon peel; season to taste with salt and pepper. Drizzle mixture over arranged salad. Marinate salad in refrigerator 1 to 2 hours. Garnish with parsley or cilantro sprigs, if desired.

Makes 4 servings

Favorite recipe from ***Washington Apple Commission***

Corn Pudding Soufflé

HICKORY BEEF KABOBS

- 1 pound boneless beef top sirloin or tenderloin steak, cut into 1¼-inch pieces
- 4 small ears thawed frozen corn, cut into 1-inch pieces
- 1 green or red bell pepper, cut into 1-inch pieces
- 1 small red onion, cut into ½-inch wedges
- ½ cup beer or nonalcoholic beer
- ½ cup chili sauce
- 1 teaspoon dry mustard
- 2 cloves garlic, minced
- 1½ cups hickory chips
- Hot cooked rice (optional)

Place beef and vegetables in plastic bag. Combine next 4 ingredients in bowl; pour into bag. Seal; turn to coat. Refrigerate 1 to 8 hours; turn occasionally. Soak hickory chips in cold water 20 minutes. Drain beef and vegetables; reserve marinade. Alternately thread beef and vegetables onto skewers. Brush with marinade. Drain chips; sprinkle over medium-hot coals. Grill kabobs 10 to 12 minutes or until desir d doneness. Brush with marinade and turn over once; discard remaining marinade. Serve over rice.

Makes 4 servings

STUFFED PORK CHOPS

- 4 rib pork chops, cut 1¼ inches thick, slit for stuffing
- 1½ cups prepared stuffing
- 1 tablespoon vegetable oil
- Salt and pepper
- 1 bottle (12 ounces) HEINZ® Chili Sauce

Trim excess fat from chops. Place stuffing in pockets of chops; secure with wooden toothpicks or string. In large skillet, brown chops in oil; season with salt and pepper. Place chops in 2-quart oblong baking dish. Pour chili sauce over chops. Cover with foil; bake in 350°F oven 30 minutes. Stir sauce; turn and baste chops. Cover; bake an additional 30 to 40 minutes or until chops are cooked. Remove toothpicks. Skim excess fat. Spoon sauce over chops. *Makes 4 servings*

RANGE TOP COOKING DIRECTIONS: Stuff and brown chops as above. Drain excess fat. Season chops with salt and pepper; pour chili sauce over. Cook, covered, 30 minutes, turning chops and basting halfway through cooking. Remove toothpicks from chops. Skim excess fat from sauce.

STROGANOFF NOODLES & MEATBALLS

- ½ pound ground beef or turkey
- ¼ cup Italian-style dry bread crumbs
- 1 tablespoon water
- 1 tablespoon vegetable or olive oil
- 1½ cups water
- ½ cup milk
- 1 package LIPTON® Noodles & Sauce–Stroganoff
- 1 jar (4½ ounces) sliced mushrooms, drained
- 1 teaspoon chopped fresh parsley*

*Substitution: Use ½ teaspoon dried parsley flakes.

In medium bowl, combine ground beef, bread crumbs and 1 tablespoon water. Shape into sixteen 1-inch meatballs. In 10-inch skillet, heat oil and cook meatballs over medium heat 5 minutes or until done; set aside.

In medium saucepan, bring 1½ cups water and milk to the boiling point. Stir in Noodles & Stroganoff Sauce and continue boiling over medium heat, stirring occasionally, 7 minutes. Stir in mushrooms, parsley and meatballs and continue cooking, stirring frequently, 3 minutes or until noodles are tender. *Makes 2 (2-cup) servings*

Stuffed Pork Chop

PATCHWORK CASSEROLE

- **2 pounds ground beef**
- **2 cups chopped green bell pepper**
- **1 cup chopped onion**
- **2 pounds frozen Southern-style hash-brown potatoes, thawed**
- **2 cans (8 ounces each) tomato sauce**
- **1 cup water**
- **1 can (6 ounces) tomato paste**
- **1 teaspoon salt**
- **½ teaspoon dried basil, crumbled**
- **¼ teaspoon ground black pepper**
- **1 pound pasteurized process American cheese, thinly sliced**

Preheat oven to 350°F.

Cook and stir beef in large skillet over medium heat until crumbled and brown, about 10 minutes; drain off fat.

Add green pepper and onion; cook and stir until tender, about 4 minutes. Stir in potatoes, tomato sauce, water, tomato paste, salt, basil and black pepper.

Spoon ½ mixture into 13×9×2-inch baking pan or 3-quart baking dish; top with half of cheese. Spoon remaining meat mixture evenly on top of cheese. Cover pan with aluminum foil. Bake 45 minutes.

Cut remaining cheese into decorative shapes; place on top of casserole. Let stand loosely covered until cheese melts, about 5 minutes.

Makes 8 to 10 servings

BAKED COUNTRY CURED HAM

- **1 country cured ham, 10 to 14 pounds**
- **Whole cloves**
- **6 cups hot water**
- **1 cup vinegar**
- **1 cup cider**
- **1 tablespoon Worcestershire sauce**
- **2 bay leaves**
- **1 cup molasses**

Remove rind or skin from ham without removing the delicate layer of fat. Gently wash ham under running water. Pat dry and score fat into diamond shapes. Place a whole clove in each diamond. Insert meat thermometer into meaty part of ham, being careful not to touch fat or bone. Place ham, fat side up, in large roasting pan with cover. Use heavy duty aluminum foil to make a cover, if necessary. In large bowl, combine water, vinegar, cider and Worcestershire sauce; pour over ham. Place bay leaves in liquid. Bake at 325°F 20 minutes per pound or to an internal temperature of 160°F. Baste often during cooking time with molasses. Bake uncovered last 30 minutes. Decorate with fruit, if desired. Cool before slicing.

Makes 20 to 25 servings

Favorite recipe from ***National Pork Producers Council***

Patchwork Casserole

PORK CHOPS IN RAISIN SAUCE

2 pork chops, thick cut
1 large clove garlic, minced
Salt and pepper (optional)
1 teaspoon olive oil
½ teaspoon thyme, crumbled
¼ teaspoon sage
1 cup orange juice, divided
2 teaspoons cornstarch
½ cup DOLE® Raisins

- Rub pork chops with garlic. Sprinkle with salt and pepper, if desired.
- In nonstick skillet, brown chops in oil. Cover skillet during browning. Add thyme and sage; stir into pan juices.
- Mix 3 tablespoons orange juice with cornstarch. Set aside. Add remaining juice to skillet. Cover; simmer 10 minutes.
- Stir in cornstarch mixture until blended. Add raisins. Cook, stirring constantly, until sauce boils and thickens. *Makes 2 servings*

SUNDAY ROAST BEEF

1 (7½-pound) heavy, aged ribeye roast, about 4 inches thick at thickest part
3 tablespoons Chef Paul Prudhomme's BLACKENED STEAK MAGIC®
1½ teaspoons dry mustard
6 tablespoons unsalted butter
1¼ cups finely chopped onions
1¼ cups finely chopped celery
1¼ cups finely chopped green bell peppers
2 teaspoons minced garlic

Preheat oven to 300°F. Trim fat cap to ¼-inch thickness. Lay roast, fat side up, in 15×11-inch roasting pan without rack.

Combine Blackened Steak Magic® and mustard in small bowl.

Melt butter over medium heat in large, heavy skillet. Add Blackened Steak Magic® mixture, onions, celery and bell peppers; stir to coat vegetables well. Cook and stir 2½ minutes. Add garlic. Cook 1½ minutes more, stirring and scraping pan bottom well. Remove from heat and pour mixture into glass bowl to stop cooking.

Starting at one end of roast, cut about eleven 2-inch slits (about 2 fingers wide) down length of roast to form pockets, being careful not to cut through to bottom. Stuff each pocket with 1 rounded tablespoon of the mixture; carefully turn roast back to fat side up and cover tip and sides with remaining vegetable mixture. Bake uncovered at 300° for 1 hour 30 minutes for rare or 1 hour 40 minutes for medium rare. (Note: If the roast you purchase is flatter than 4 inches thick, you'll need to check the internal temperature with thermometer probe after about 1 hour 15 minutes. A true rare will register 127°F, medium-rare 138°F, medium 148°F, medium-well 158°F—any temperature in excess of 165°F is considered well done, which is not recommended for fine cuts of beef.) Remove from oven and transfer roast to cutting board or platter; let sit 15 to 20 minutes before carving.

Makes 10 to 12 servings

CORN BREAD AND BACON BATTER BAKE

1 (7½-ounce) package corn bread mix, plus ingredients to prepare mix
2 ARMOUR® Lower Salt Jumbo Meat Hot Dogs, cut crosswise into thirds
3 slices ARMOUR® Lower Salt Bacon, cooked crisp and crumbled
½ cup (2 ounces) shredded ARMOUR® Lower Salt Cheddar Cheese

Preheat oven to 400°F. Prepare corn bread mix according to package directions. Spray 10-inch ovenproof skillet or 8×8-inch baking pan with nonstick cooking spray; pour in batter. Stand hot dog piece on 1 end. Cut down into hot dog almost to the end. (Do not cut all the way through.) Make another cut into hot dog, like the first, to form crisscross. Repeat with all hot dog pieces. Place hot dogs cut side up into batter 2 inches from side of pan, arranging in circle. Bake about 18 to 25 minutes, or until toothpick inserted in center of corn bread comes out clean. Sprinkle bacon and cheese over top. Let stand for 5 minutes before serving.

Makes 6 servings

SAVORY POT ROAST

1 (2½-pound) bottom round roast
1 tablespoon vegetable oil
½ cup A.1.® Steak Sauce
½ cup ketchup
½ cup red wine vinegar
1 teaspoon dry mustard
1 teaspoon garlic powder

In Dutch oven, over medium-high heat, brown roast in hot oil; drain.

Blend steak sauce, ketchup, vinegar, mustard and garlic powder; pour over meat. Heat to a boil; reduce heat. Cover and simmer 2½ to 3 hours or until meat is fork-tender, skimming and discarding excess fat as necessary. Slice roast and serve with pan gravy. Garnish as desired.

Makes 6 servings

BUTTERFLIED SOUTHERN CITRUS BARBECUE

6 to 9 pounds butterflied leg of lamb
1½ cups grapefruit juice
3 tablespoons brown sugar
1 tablespoon grated grapefruit or lemon peel
2 cloves garlic, minced
1 teaspoon ground cloves
1 teaspoon ground allspice
½ teaspoon salt
¼ teaspoon ground pepper
Few drops hot pepper sauce

Place lamb in large glass or enamel bowl. In measuring cup, combine remaining ingredients. Pour over lamb. Cover and refrigerate several hours or overnight. Drain lamb, reserving marinade. Grill lamb 4 to 6 inches above coals or source of heat for 1 hour and 15 minutes or until meat thermometer inserted in thickest part registers 140°F for rare or 150°F to 155°F for medium. Baste with marinade.

Makes 8 servings

Favorite recipe from ***American Lamb Council***

SPAGHETTI WITH MEATBALLS

1½ pounds lean ground beef
1 cup finely chopped onion
¾ cup grated Parmesan cheese
½ cup fresh bread crumbs (1 slice)
3 cups tomato juice
4 teaspoons WYLER'S® or STEERO® Beef-Flavor Instant Bouillon
2½ teaspoons Italian seasoning
2 cloves garlic, finely chopped
8 ounces fresh mushrooms, sliced (about 2 cups)
1 (6-ounce) can tomato paste
1½ teaspoons sugar
1 (1-pound) package CREAMETTE® Spaghetti, cooked as package directs and drained

In large bowl, combine meat, *½ cup* onion, cheese, crumbs, *½ cup* tomato juice, *2 teaspoons* bouillon and *1¼ teaspoons* Italian seasoning; mix well. Shape into meatballs. In large kettle or Dutch oven, brown meatballs; remove from pan. In same pan, cook remaining *½ cup* onion, garlic and mushrooms until tender. Stir in remaining *2½ cups* tomato juice, tomato paste, sugar, remaining *2 teaspoons* bouillon and *1¼ teaspoons* Italian seasoning. Add meatballs; simmer uncovered 30 to 40 minutes. Serve with hot spaghetti. Refrigerate leftovers.

Makes 6 to 8 servings

Butterflied Southern Citrus Barbecue

TEXAS-STYLE DEEP-DISH CHILI PIE

- **1 pound beef stew meat, cut into ½-inch cubes**
- **1 tablespoon vegetable oil**
- **2 cans (14½ ounces *each*) Mexican-style stewed tomatoes, undrained**
- **1 medium green bell pepper, diced**
- **1 package (1.25 ounces) LAWRY'S® Taco Spices & Seasonings**
- **1 tablespoon yellow cornmeal**
- **1 can (15¼ ounces) kidney beans, drained**
- **1 package (15 ounces) flat refrigerated pie crusts**
- **½ cup (2 ounces) shredded Cheddar cheese, divided**

In Dutch oven, brown beef in oil; drain fat. Add stewed tomatoes, bell pepper, Taco Spices & Seasonings and cornmeal. Bring to a boil; reduce heat and simmer, uncovered, 20 minutes. Add kidney beans.

In 10-inch pie plate, unfold 1 crust and fill with chili mixture and ¼ cup cheese. Top with remaining crust, fluting edges. Bake, uncovered, in 350°F oven 30 minutes. Sprinkle remaining cheese over crust; return to oven and bake 10 minutes longer. *Makes 6 servings*

PORK ROAST WITH CORN BREAD & OYSTER STUFFING

- **1 (5- to 7-pound) pork loin roast***
- **2 tablespoons butter or margarine**
- **½ cup chopped onion**
- **½ cup chopped celery**
- **2 cloves garlic, minced**
- **½ teaspoon fennel seeds, crushed**
- **1 teaspoon TABASCO® pepper sauce**
- **½ teaspoon salt**
- **2 cups packaged corn bread stuffing mix**
- **1 can (8 ounces) oysters, undrained, chopped**

*Have butcher crack backbone of pork loin roast.

Preheat oven to 325°F. Make a deep slit in back of each chop on pork loin. In large saucepan, melt butter; add onion, celery, garlic and fennel seeds. Cook 5 minutes or until vegetables are tender; stir in TABASCO sauce and salt. Add stuffing mix, oysters and oyster liquid; toss to mix well.

Stuff corn bread mixture into slits in pork. (Any leftover stuffing may be baked in covered baking dish during last 30 minutes of roasting.) Place meat in shallow roasting pan. Cook 30 to 35 minutes per pound or until meat thermometer inserted into meat registers 170°F. Remove to heated serving platter. Allow meat to stand 15 minutes before serving.

Makes 10 to 12 servings

Texas-Style Deep-Dish Chili Pie

SAUSAGE SKILLET DINNER

12 ounces fully cooked smoked pork link sausage, cut diagonally into 1-inch pieces
2 tablespoons water
1 medium onion
2 small red apples
2 tablespoons butter, divided
12 ounces natural frozen potato wedges
¼ cup cider vinegar
3 tablespoons sugar
½ teaspoon caraway seeds
2 tablespoons chopped fresh parsley

Place sausage and water in large nonstick skillet; cover tightly and cook over medium heat 8 minutes, stirring occasionally. Meanwhile, cut onion into 12 wedges; core and cut each apple into 8 wedges. Remove sausage to warm platter. Pour off drippings. Cook and stir onion and apples in 1 tablespoon of butter in same skillet, 4 minutes or until apples are crisp-tender. Remove to sausage platter.

Heat remaining 1 tablespoon butter; add potatoes and cook, covered, over medium-high heat 5 minutes or until potatoes are tender and golden brown, stirring occasionally. Combine vinegar, sugar and caraway seeds. Reduce heat; return sausage, apple mixture and vinegar mixture to skillet. Cook 1 minute or until heated through, stirring gently. Sprinkle with parsley.

Makes 4 servings

Favorite recipe from ***National Live Stock & Meat Board***

CORNED BEEF, POTATO AND PEPPER HASH

Water
1 teaspoon salt
1 pound Russet potatoes, cut into ½-inch cubes
2 tablespoons butter, divided
1 medium onion, coarsely chopped
⅓ cup *each* chopped red, yellow and green bell peppers
12 ounces cooked corned beef, cut into ½-inch cubes
3 tablespoons chopped parsley
¼ cup half-and-half
3 tablespoons dry white wine
½ teaspoon dry mustard
⅛ teaspoon black pepper

Bring water to a boil in large saucepan; add salt and potatoes. Return to a boil. Cook 5 minutes; drain well. Melt 1 tablespoon butter in cast-iron or large heavy skillet over medium-high heat; add onion and bell peppers. Cook and stir 2 minutes or until crisp-tender; remove from pan. Add corned beef, potatoes and parsley to onion mixture; mix lightly. Combine half-and-half, wine, mustard and pepper; add to corned beef mixture and mix well. Wipe out cast-iron skillet with paper towel; place over medium heat until hot. Add remaining butter. Add beef mixture, pressing down firmly. Cook 15 minutes or until browned; turn with spatula several times.

Makes 4 servings

Favorite recipe from ***National Live Stock & Meat Board***

Sausage Skillet Dinner

STRING PIE

- 1 pound ground beef
- ½ cup chopped onion
- ¼ cup chopped green pepper
- 1 jar (15½ ounces) spaghetti sauce
- 8 ounces spaghetti, cooked and drained
- ⅓ cup grated Parmesan cheese
- 2 eggs, beaten
- 2 teaspoons butter
- 1 cup cottage cheese
- ½ cup (2 ounces) shredded mozzarella cheese

Cook beef, onion and green pepper in large skillet over medium-high heat until meat is brown, stirring to separate meat. Drain fat. Stir in spaghetti sauce; mix well. Combine spaghetti, Parmesan cheese, eggs and butter in large bowl; mix well. Place in bottom of 13×9-inch pan. Spread cottage cheese over top. Pour sauce mixture over cottage cheese. Sprinkle mozzarella cheese over top. Bake in preheated 350°F oven until cheese melts, about 20 minutes.

Makes 6 to 8 servings

Favorite recipe from ***North Dakota Beef Commission***

HAM WITH FRUITED MUSTARD SAUCE

- 1 fully cooked ham slice (1 to 1¼ pounds), cut ½ inch thick*
- 1 tablespoon butter or margarine
- 1 can (8 ounces) pineapple slices, undrained
- ¼ cup HEINZ® 57 Sauce
- 2 tablespoons honey
- 1 tablespoon prepared mustard
- 1½ teaspoons cornstarch
- Dash ground allspice

*A 1-pound piece of Canadian bacon, cut into 4 slices, may be substituted.

Cut ham into 4 serving portions. In large skillet, cook ham in butter 3 to 4 minutes on each side or until heated through. Meanwhile, drain pineapple, reserving juice. In small bowl, combine juice, 57 Sauce, honey, mustard, cornstarch and allspice. Remove ham from skillet; keep warm. Pour 57 Sauce mixture into skillet and cook until thickened. Return ham to skillet. Top each ham portion with pineapple slice and spoon sauce over; heat through.

Makes 4 servings (about ⅔ cups sauce)

String Pie

WESTERN LAMB RIBLETS

5 pounds lamb riblets, cut into serving-size pieces
¾ cup chili sauce
½ cup honey
½ cup beer
¼ cup Worcestershire sauce
¼ cup finely chopped onion
1 clove garlic, minced
½ teaspoon crushed red pepper

Trim excess fat from riblets. In saucepan combine chili sauce, honey, beer, Worcestershire, onion, garlic and red pepper; heat mixture to boiling. Reduce heat; simmer, covered, 10 minutes. Remove from heat; cool.

Place riblets in plastic bag; pour marinade over riblets. Close bag; set bag in large bowl. Marinate riblets in refrigerator about 2 hours, turning bag occasionally to distribute marinade evenly.

Drain riblets; reserve marinade. Arrange medium-hot KINGSFORD® briquets around drip pan. Place riblets over drip pan. Cover grill and cook 45 minutes, turning riblets and brushing with marinade twice. Heat remaining marinade and serve with riblets. *Makes 6 servings*

LENTIL AND SAUSAGE RAGOUT

1 pound ECKRICH® Beef Smoked Sausage, cut into ¼-inch slices
2 large onions, sliced
3 tablespoons vegetable oil
2 large cloves garlic, minced
3 cans (14½ ounces each) stewed tomatoes, undrained
1½ teaspoons paprika
1 teaspoon dried thyme leaves
1 teaspoon dried marjoram leaves
Dash ground black pepper
4 cups water
1 cup dried lentils, sorted, rinsed
2 ribs celery, chopped
¼ cup chopped fresh parsley (optional)

Cook and stir onions in oil in large saucepan over medium heat until lightly browned. Add garlic, tomatoes with juice, paprika, thyme, marjoram and pepper. Bring to a boil over high heat. Reduce heat to low; simmer 10 minutes. Add sausage to tomato mixture; simmer 20 minutes. In separate saucepan, combine water, lentils and celery. Bring to a boil over high heat. Reduce heat to low; cover and simmer 20 minutes or until lentils are tender. Drain; add to tomato mixture. Heat until hot. Garnish with parsley. *Makes 8 to 10 servings*

Pork Roast with Sausage & Spinach Stuffing

1 envelope LIPTON® Recipe Secrets® Onion, Onion-Mushroom or Beefy Mushroom Soup Mix
1 package (10 ounces) frozen chopped spinach, cooked and drained
½ pound sweet Italian sausage links, removed from casing
½ cup fresh bread crumbs
½ cup slivered almonds, toasted
2 eggs, slightly beaten
2 tablespoons finely chopped fresh parsley
2 teaspoons dried thyme leaves, divided
1 teaspoon finely chopped garlic (about 1 medium clove), divided
⅛ teaspoon pepper
1 (2½-pound) boneless center cut pork loin roast
1 to 2 tablespoons vegetable oil

Preheat oven to 350°F.

In large bowl, thoroughly combine onion soup mix, spinach, sausage, bread crumbs, almonds, eggs, parsley, 1 teaspoon thyme, ½ teaspoon garlic and pepper; set aside.

Butterfly roast as directed. Spread spinach mixture evenly on cut side of roast. Roll, starting at longest side, and tie securely with string. In roasting pan, on rack, place pork seam side down. Rub roast with oil, then top with remaining garlic and thyme. Roast 1½ hours or until meat thermometer reaches 165°F (medium) or 180°F (well done).

Makes about 8 servings

TO BUTTERFLY A PORK LOIN ROAST:

1. Place boneless roast fat side down. Starting at the thickest edge, slice horizontally through the meat stopping 1 inch from the opposite edge so that the roast can open like a book.

2. Lightly pound the opened roast and remove any fat thicker than ¼ inch.

Souperior Meat Loaf

1 envelope LIPTON® Recipe Secrets® Onion Soup Mix*
2 pounds ground beef
1½ cups fresh bread crumbs
2 eggs
¾ cup water
⅓ cup ketchup

*Also terrific with LIPTON® Recipe Secrets® Beefy Onion, Onion-Mushroom, Italian Herb with Tomato or Savory Herb with Garlic Soup Mix.

Preheat oven to 350°F.

In large bowl, combine soup mix, beef, bread crumbs, eggs, water and ketchup. In 13×9-inch baking dish or roasting pan, shape into loaf. Bake 1 hour or until done. Let stand 10 minutes before serving.

Makes 8 servings

T-BONE STEAKS WITH VEGETABLE KABOBS

4 beef T-bone steaks, cut 1 to 1½ inches thick
Salt and pepper
Vegetable Kabobs (recipe follows)

Grill steaks over medium coals. When first sides are browned, turn and season with salt and pepper; finish cooking second sides. Turn and season. Steaks cut 1 inch thick require about 16 minutes for rare; 20 minutes for medium. Steaks cut 1½ inches thick require about 22 minutes for rare; 30 minutes for medium. Serve with Vegetable Kabobs. *Makes 4 servings*

Vegetable Kabobs

2 large potatoes (about 1½ pounds)
1 large sweet onion
3 tablespoons butter, melted
1 teaspoon paprika
½ teaspoon celery salt
¼ teaspoon garlic powder
⅛ teaspoon freshly ground pepper

Cook potatoes (do not peel) in boiling salted water 20 minutes; drain. Cut each potato crosswise into four 1-inch-thick slices. Cut onion crosswise into four 1-inch-thick slices. Alternately thread 2 potato slices and 1 onion slice, through skin of vegetables, on each of four 8-inch skewers. Combine butter, paprika, celery salt, garlic powder and pepper. Brush both sides of vegetables with seasoned butter. Grill kabobs over medium coals 20 minutes, turning after 10 minutes and brushing with seasoned butter occasionally.

Makes 4 servings

Favorite recipe from ***National Live Stock & Meat Board***

FAMILY BAKED BEAN DINNER

1 can (20 ounces) DOLE® Pineapple Chunks in Juice
½ DOLE® Green Bell Pepper, julienne-cut
½ cup chopped onion
1 pound Polish sausage or frankfurters, cut into 1-inch chunks
⅓ cup packed brown sugar
1 teaspoon dry mustard
2 cans (16 ounces each) baked beans

- **MICROWAVE DIRECTIONS:** Drain pineapple; reserve juice for beverage. Add green pepper and onion to 13×9-inch microwavable dish.
- Cover; microwave on HIGH (100% power) 3 minutes. Add sausage, arranging around edges of dish. Cover; continue microwaving on HIGH (100% power) 6 minutes.
- In bowl, combine brown sugar and mustard; stir in beans and pineapple. Add to sausage mixture. Stir to combine. Microwave, uncovered, on HIGH (100% power) 8 to 10 minutes, stirring after 4 minutes. *Makes 6 servings*

T-Bone Steaks with Vegetable Kabobs

LAMB & PORK CASSOULET

- 1 package (1 pound) dry white navy beans, rinsed
- Water
- ½ pound salt pork, sliced
- 1½ pounds boneless lamb shoulder or leg, cut into 1-inch cubes
- 4 large pork chops
- ½ pound pork sausages
- Salt
- Pepper
- 2 large onions, chopped
- 1 can (28 ounces) tomatoes, drained
- ½ cup dry red wine
- 3 cloves garlic, finely chopped
- ¼ cup chopped fresh parsley
- 1 teaspoon dried thyme, crushed
- 1 bay leaf

Place beans in large bowl. Cover with cold water; soak overnight. Drain and rinse beans. Place beans in Dutch oven; cover with cold water. Bring to a boil over high heat. Skim foam as necessary. Reduce heat to low. Cover and simmer about 1 hour. Drain beans, reserving liquid.

Fry salt pork in large skillet over medium-high heat until some of the fat is rendered. Remove salt pork. In batches, brown lamb, pork chops and sausages in fat. Remove from skillet; drain on paper towels. Cut chops and sausages into 1-inch pieces. Sprinkle meat with salt and pepper. Remove all but 2 tablespoons of the fat from skillet. Add onions. Cook and stir over medium-high heat until onions are tender. Add tomatoes, wine, garlic, parsley, thyme and bay leaf. Combine tomato mixture, drained beans and meats in large bowl. Spoon into large casserole. Pour reserved bean liquid over mixture just to cover. Bake at 350°F about 1½ hours or until meat is fork-tender. Remove bay leaf before serving.

Makes 6 to 8 servings

Favorite recipe from ***American Lamb Council***

SPICY BARBECUE BEEF

- ½ cup A.1.® Steak Sauce
- ⅓ cup chili sauce
- 3 tablespoons GREY POUPON® Dijon Mustard
- ¼ cup water
- 1 pound beef top round steak
- 1 tablespoon vegetable oil
- 1 large onion, sliced
- Hot cooked wide noodles (optional)

In small bowl, combine steak sauce, chili sauce, mustard and water; set aside.

In large skillet, over medium-high heat, brown steak in oil. Add onion, stirring until lightly browned. Stir in sauce mixture; heat to a boil. Cover; reduce heat and simmer 1½ hours or until steak is tender. Slice steak and serve with noodles if desired. *Makes 4 servings*

Lamb & Pork Cassoulet

TEXAS-STYLE BEEF BRISKET

6 to 8 pounds boneless beef brisket
¾ cup finely chopped onion
2 teaspoons paprika
½ teaspoon freshly ground pepper
Water
1 cup prepared steak sauce
Special Sauce (recipe follows)

Trim fat covering on brisket to ¼ inch. Combine onion, paprika and pepper. Rub mixture evenly over surface of brisket. Place brisket, fat side up, in large disposable aluminum pan. Add ½ cup water. Cover pan tightly with aluminum foil. Place in center of grid over very low coals. (Single layer of coals with space in between each.) Place cover on cooker and cook 5 hours, turning brisket over every 1½ hours. (Remove fat from pan with baster as it accumulates.) Add ½ cup water, as needed, to pan. (Be sure to add briquets as needed to keep coals at very low temperature.)

Remove foil from pan. Remove brisket; place on grid directly over very low coals. Combine pan drippings with steak sauce; reserve 1 cup for Special Sauce. Brush part of remaining steak sauce mixture over brisket. Replace cover and continue cooking 1 hour, brushing occasionally with steak sauce mixture. Serve brisket with Special Sauce.
Makes 24 to 30 servings

Special Sauce: Cook ½ cup finely chopped onion in 2 tablespoons butter until tender. Stir in 1 cup reserved steak sauce/beef drippings mixture, 1 cup ketchup, 1 tablespoon brown sugar and ¼ to ½ teaspoon crushed red pepper. Simmer 10 minutes.
Makes 2 cups

Favorite recipe from ***National Live Stock & Meat Board***

SHEPHERD'S PIE

2 cups diced cooked leg of American lamb
2 large potatoes, cubed and cooked
3 green onions, sliced
1 cup cooked peas
1 cup cooked carrot slices
1 clove garlic, minced
2 cups prepared brown gravy
1 teaspoon black pepper
2 sheets prepared pie dough*

*Or, use mashed potatoes on top in place of second crust.

In large bowl, combine lamb, potatoes, green onions, peas, carrots, garlic, brown gravy and black pepper.

Place 1 sheet pie dough in pie plate; fill with lamb mixture. Cover with second sheet of pie dough. Crimp edges; cut slits in top to allow steam to escape.

Bake 30 minutes at 350°F or until pie crust is golden brown. *Makes 4 to 6 servings*

Favorite recipe from ***American Lamb Council***

Texas-Style Beef Brisket

CHICKEN AND HAM WITH RICE

- **¾ pound boned chicken breasts, cut into strips**
- **4 ounces boiled ham, cut into strips**
- **2 tablespoons butter or margarine**
- **1 can (10¾ ounces) condensed cream of chicken soup**
- **1 cup water**
- **2 tablespoons Dijon-style mustard (optional)**
- **1 package (10 ounces) asparagus cuts, thawed**
- **1½ cups MINUTE® Rice**
- **2 slices Swiss cheese, cut into wedges or small cubes**

• Cook and stir chicken and ham in hot butter in large skillet until lightly browned.

• Stir in soup, water and mustard; add asparagus. Bring to a boil. Stir in rice and top with cheese. Cover; remove from heat.

• Let stand 5 minutes. Fluff with fork.

Makes 4 servings

TASTY TURKEY POT PIE

½ cup MIRACLE WHIP® Salad Dressing
2 tablespoons flour
1 teaspoon instant chicken bouillon
⅛ teaspoon pepper
¾ cup milk
1½ cups chopped cooked turkey or chicken
1 (10-ounce) package frozen mixed vegetables, thawed, drained
1 (4-ounce) can refrigerated crescent rolls

- Combine salad dressing, flour, bouillon and pepper in medium saucepan. Gradually add milk.
- Cook, stirring constantly, over low heat until thickened. Add turkey and vegetables; heat thoroughly, stirring occasionally.
- Spoon into 8-inch square baking dish. Unroll dough into two rectangles. Press perforations together to seal. Place rectangles side-by-side to form square; press edges together to form seam. Cover turkey mixture with dough.
- Bake at 375°F 15 to 20 minutes or until browned. *Makes 4 to 6 servings*

Preparation Time: 15 minutes
Baking Time: 20 minutes

VARIATIONS: Combine 1 egg, beaten and 1 tablespoon cold water, mixing until well blended. Brush dough with egg mixture just before baking.

Substitute one chicken bouillon cube for instant chicken bouillon.

Substitute 10×6-inch baking dish for 8-inch square baking dish.

Substitute 12×8-inch baking dish for 8-inch square dish. Double all ingredients. Assemble recipe as directed, using three dough rectangles to form top crust. Decorate crust with cutouts from remaining rectangle. Bake as directed.

MICROWAVE TIP: To prepare sauce, combine salad dressing, flour, bouillon and pepper in 1-quart microwavable measure or bowl; gradually add milk. Microwave on HIGH 4 to 5 minutes or until thickened, stirring after each minute.

Tasty Turkey Pot Pie

Chicken Skillet Supper

- 1½ teaspoons salt
- ¼ teaspoon pepper
- ¼ teaspoon ground paprika
- ⅛ teaspoon garlic powder
- 1 broiler-fryer chicken (about 3 pounds), cut into serving pieces
- 1 tablespoon vegetable oil
- 2 tablespoons water
- 1 medium onion, chopped
- 1 medium potato, peeled, cut into 2¼-inch strips
- 1 tablespoon slivered almonds (optional)
- 1 can (8 ounces) tomato sauce
- 1 cup chicken broth
- 1 teaspoon sugar
- 1 package (10 ounces) frozen French-cut green beans or mixed vegetables

Mix salt, pepper, paprika and garlic powder in small bowl; rub over chicken. Heat oil in large skillet over medium heat; add chicken, skin-side down. Cover and cook 10 minutes. Add water to chicken; cover and cook 30 minutes longer, turning chicken over every 10 minutes. Remove chicken from skillet; reserve.

Add onion, potato and almonds to drippings in skillet; cook until onion is tender, about 3 minutes. Add tomato sauce, broth and sugar to onion mixture; cook until liquid comes to a boil. Add beans and chicken pieces to tomato mixture; cover and cook until beans are tender, about 10 minutes. Serve hot. *Makes 4 to 6 servings*

Hearty Bistro Chicken

- 2 tablespoons olive or vegetable oil
- 2½- to 3-pound chicken, cut into serving pieces
- 2 ears fresh or frozen corn, cut into 1½-inch pieces
- 1 package (8 ounces) frozen snap peas
- 1 cup frozen sliced carrots
- 1 envelope LIPTON® Recipe Secrets® Onion Soup Mix
- 2 cups water
- ¼ cup sherry (optional)
- 2 tablespoons country Dijon-style prepared mustard
- 2 tablespoons all-purpose flour
- 1 cup sour cream

In 12-inch skillet, heat oil and brown chicken over medium-high heat; drain. Add corn, peas and carrots, then onion soup mix blended with water, sherry and mustard. Bring to a boil, then simmer covered 20 minutes or until chicken is done.

Remove chicken and vegetables to serving platter and keep warm; reserve liquid. Boil reserved liquid over high heat 10 minutes. Remove from heat, then stir in flour blended with sour cream; return to heat. Bring just to the boiling point, then simmer, stirring constantly, until sauce is thickened, about 3 minutes. To serve, pour sauce over chicken and vegetables. *Makes 4 servings*

Chicken Skillet Supper

OLD-FASHIONED CHICKEN WITH DUMPLINGS

- **3 to 3½ pounds chicken pieces**
- **3 tablespoons butter or margarine**
- **2 cans (14½ ounces each) ready-to-serve chicken broth**
- **3½ cups water**
- **1 teaspoon salt**
- **¼ teaspoon white pepper**
- **2 large carrots, cut into 1-inch slices**
- **2 ribs celery, cut into 1-inch slices**
- **8 to 10 small boiling onions**
- **¼ pound small mushrooms, cut into halves**
- **Parsley Dumplings (recipe follows)**
- **½ cup frozen peas, thawed, drained**

Brown chicken in melted butter in 6- to 8-quart saucepan over medium-high heat. Add broth, water, salt and pepper. Bring to a boil over high heat. Reduce heat to low. Cover; simmer 15 minutes. Add carrots, celery, onions and mushrooms. Simmer, covered, 40 minutes or until chicken and vegetables are tender. Prepare Parsley Dumplings. When chicken is tender, skim fat from broth. Stir in peas. Drop dumpling mixture into broth, making 6 large or 12 small dumplings. Cover; simmer 15 to 20 minutes or until dumplings are firm to the touch and wooden pick inserted in center comes out clean.

Makes 6 servings

Parsley Dumplings: Sift 2 cups all-purpose flour, 4 teaspoons baking powder and ½ teaspoon salt into medium bowl. Cut in 5 tablespoons cold butter or margarine until mixture resembles coarse meal. Make a well in center; pour in 1 cup milk, all at once. Add 2 tablespoons chopped parsley; stir with fork until mixture forms a ball.

Makes 6 large or 12 small dumplings

TURKEY HASH

- **2 cups cubed cooked BUTTERBALL® Turkey (¾ pound)**
- **½ cup chopped celery**
- **⅓ cup chopped onion**
- **⅓ cup chopped green bell pepper**
- **½ stick (¼ cup) butter or margarine**
- **3 cups diced cooked potatoes**
- **½ teaspoon poultry seasoning**
- **¼ teaspoon salt**
- **⅛ teaspoon ground black pepper**
- **½ to 1 cup turkey gravy**

Cook and stir celery, onion and green pepper in butter in heavy skillet over medium heat until tender. Stir in turkey, potatoes and seasonings. Cook over low heat, about 5 minutes, stirring frequently. Add gravy and continue to cook and stir until mixture is hot.

Makes 4 servings

CHICKEN, SAUSAGE 'N' SHRIMP GUMBO

- 1 can (28 ounces) whole tomatoes, undrained
- 3 chicken breast halves, boned, skinned and cut into 1½-inch pieces
- ½ pound Creole or smoked Polish sausage, sliced ½ inch thick
- 2 bay leaves
- 1 teaspoon freshly ground black pepper
- 1 teaspoon thyme
- ⅛ to ¼ teaspoon cayenne pepper or to taste
- 2 cups chicken broth
- 1 cup UNCLE BEN'S® CONVERTED® Brand Rice
- ¾ cup coarsely chopped onion
- ¾ cup sliced celery
- 2 large garlic cloves, crushed
- ¼ cup water
- 3 tablespoons flour
- 1 pound medium shrimp, peeled and deveined
- 1 large green pepper, cut into ¾-inch squares
- ¼ cup minced parsley

Coarsely chop tomatoes, reserving juice. Combine tomatoes, juice, chicken, sausage, bay leaves, black pepper, thyme and cayenne pepper in large skillet. Bring to a boil. Reduce heat. Cover and simmer 15 minutes. Meanwhile, bring chicken broth to a boil in medium saucepan. Stir in rice, onion, celery and garlic. Cover tightly and simmer 20 minutes. Blend water with flour until smooth. Add to skillet with shrimp and green pepper. Cook, uncovered, stirring occasionally, until shrimp are cooked through and gumbo is thickened, 5 to 7 minutes. Remove rice from heat. Let stand covered until all liquid is absorbed, about 5 minutes. Stir in parsley. Remove bay leaves; discard. Divide gumbo evenly among 6 large shallow soup plates. Top each serving with rice. *Makes 6 servings*

NO-PEEK SKILLET CHICKEN

- 2 tablespoons olive or vegetable oil
- 2½- to 3-pound chicken, cut into serving pieces
- 1 can (14½ ounces) whole peeled tomatoes, undrained
- 1 jar (4½ ounces) sliced mushrooms, drained
- 1 clove garlic, minced
- 1 envelope LIPTON® Recipe Secrets® Onion Soup Mix
- Hot cooked noodles
- Chopped fresh parsley

In 12-inch skillet, heat oil and brown chicken; drain. Stir in tomatoes with juice, mushrooms and garlic combined with soup mix. Simmer, covered, 45 minutes or until chicken is tender. Serve, if desired, with hot noodles and chopped fresh parsley. *Makes about 6 servings*

HOMESPUN TURKEY 'N' VEGETABLES

1 can (14 ounces) sliced carrots, drained
1 package (9 ounces) frozen cut green beans, thawed and drained
1 can (2.8 ounces) DURKEE® French Fried Onions, divided
1 can (16 ounces) whole potatoes, drained
1 can (10¾ ounces) condensed cream of celery soup
¼ cup milk
1 tablespoon FRENCH'S® Classic Yellow Mustard
¼ teaspoon garlic powder
1 pound uncooked turkey breast slices

Preheat oven to 375°F. In 12×8-inch baking dish, combine carrots, green beans and ½ can French Fried Onions. Slice potatoes into halves; arrange as many halves as will fit, cut-side down, around edges of baking dish. Combine any remaining potatoes with vegetables in dish. In medium bowl, combine soup, milk, mustard and garlic powder; pour half of the soup mixture over vegetables. Overlap turkey slices on vegetables. Pour remaining soup mixture over turkey and potatoes. Bake, covered, at 375°F for 40 minutes or until turkey is done. Top turkey with remaining onions; bake, uncovered, 3 minutes or until onions are golden.

Makes 4 servings

BACON AND CREAMY HERB NOODLES

1 package (12 ounces) LOUIS RICH® Turkey Bacon, cut into ½-inch pieces
8 ounces fresh mushrooms, sliced
6 green onions with tops, sliced
8 ounces uncooked medium egg noodles
1 package (8 ounces) Neufchâtel or light cream cheese, cubed
⅓ cup each white wine and water *or* ⅔ cup skim milk
½ teaspoon each garlic powder, dried basil and dried thyme leaves
1 small tomato, chopped

Heat Turkey Bacon in nonstick skillet over medium heat about 10 minutes or until lightly browned, stirring frequently. Add mushrooms and onions; cook and stir an additional 4 minutes. Reserve. Meanwhile, cook noodles according to package directions in large saucepan or Dutch oven; drain. Return noodles to saucepan; add remaining ingredients except tomato. Cook and stir over medium heat until cheese melts and sauce is well blended. Add reserved Turkey Bacon mixture; toss to combine. Sprinkle with tomato before serving. Garnish as desired.

Makes 8 servings

Homespun Turkey 'n' Vegetables

CHILI TOMATO GRILLED CHICKEN

- 2 tablespoons cooking oil
- ½ cup finely chopped onion
- 1 clove garlic, minced
- 1 chicken bouillon cube
- ½ cup hot water
- 1 can (8 ounces) taco sauce or tomato sauce
- 1 teaspoon salt
- ¼ teaspoon dried oregano leaves
- 2 tablespoons vinegar
- 1 tablespoon prepared mustard
- 4 to 6 broiler-fryer chicken quarters
- 1 tablespoon mild chili powder

In small skillet, heat oil to medium temperature. Add onion and garlic; cook and stir about 3 minutes or until onion is tender. Dissolve bouillon cube in hot water; add bouillon, taco sauce, salt, oregano, vinegar and mustard to skillet. Dip chicken into sauce mixture, then lightly sprinkle chili powder on all sides of quarters. Add remaining chili powder to sauce; bring to a boil and remove from heat.

Just before grilling, dip each chicken quarter in sauce again. Cook on charcoal grill 45 to 60 minutes or until chicken can easily be pierced with fork (the white meat will be done before the dark). Turn every 10 minutes during grilling, basting with sauce during last half of grilling time.

Makes 4 to 6 servings

Favorite recipe from ***National Broiler Council***

TURKEY WILD RICE CASSEROLE

- 2 cups cubed cooked BUTTERBALL® Turkey (¾ pound)
- 1 package (6 ounces) long grain and wild rice mix
- 1 jar (2½ ounces) sliced mushrooms, drained
- ¼ cup coarsely shredded carrot
- ¼ cup finely chopped broccoli
- 1 cup (4 ounces) shredded Swiss cheese, divided
- ¾ cup half-and-half
- 2 tablespoons sherry
- ¼ teaspoon ground black pepper
- Grated Parmesan cheese
- 2 tablespoons sliced green onions

Preheat oven to 350°F. Prepare rice according to package directions. Combine turkey, rice, mushrooms, carrot, broccoli and ½ cup Swiss cheese in 2-quart baking dish. Combine half-and-half, sherry and pepper. Fold into turkey mixture. Cover with remaining ½ cup Swiss cheese. Sprinkle with Parmesan cheese. Bake in oven 30 to 40 minutes or until hot and bubbly. Top with green onions. Sprinkle with additional Parmesan cheese, if desired.

Makes 5 to 6 servings

Chili Tomato Grilled Chicken

DOWN-HOME CORN AND CHICKEN CASSEROLE

2 chickens (2 to 3 pounds each), each cut into 10 pieces
3 tablespoons Chef Paul Prudhomme's POULTRY MAGIC®, in all
⅓ cup vegetable oil
8 cups fresh corn, cut off cob (about twelve 8-inch ears), in all
3½ cups finely chopped onions
1½ cups finely chopped green bell peppers
1 pound tomatoes, peeled, chopped
3½ cups water
2 cups uncooked rice

Remove excess fat from chickens; season chicken pieces with 2 tablespoons of the Poultry Magic® and place in plastic bag. Seal and refrigerate overnight.

Heat oil in an 8-quart roasting pan over high heat until it just starts to smoke, about 6 minutes. Add the 10 largest pieces of chicken (skin side down first) and brown, cooking 5 minutes on each side. Remove chicken and reheat oil about 1 minute or until oil stops sizzling. Brown remaining chicken 5 minutes on each side. Remove and keep warm.

Add half of corn to hot oil. Scrape bottom of pan well to get up all browned chicken bits and stir to mix well. Let corn cook, without stirring, about 6 minutes. You want it to brown and to start breaking down starch. Add ½ tablespoon Poultry Magic® and stir to combine. Let mixture cook, without stirring, about 7 minutes to continue browning process. Stir in onions, bell peppers and remaining ½ tablespoon Poultry Magic®. Cover with tight-fitting lid and cook about 5 minutes. Add remaining corn and tomatoes. Stir to mix well; cover and cook 10 minutes. Transfer corn mixture to another pan and keep warm. Preheat oven to 400°F.

Add water and rice to roasting pan. Bring to a boil, stirring occasionally. Layer chicken pieces on top of rice and cover chicken layer with corn mixture. Cover and bake 25 minutes.

Remove casserole from oven. Let stand 10 minutes, covered, then serve. *Makes 8 servings*

Down-Home Corn and Chicken Casserole

TURKEY COTTAGE PIE

¼ cup butter or margarine
¼ cup all-purpose flour
1 envelope LIPTON® Recipe Secrets® Golden Onion Soup Mix
2 cups water
2 cups cut-up cooked turkey or chicken
1 package (10 ounces) frozen mixed vegetables, thawed
1¼ cups shredded Swiss cheese (about 5 ounces), divided
⅛ teaspoon pepper
5 cups hot mashed potatoes

Preheat oven to 375°F.

In large saucepan, melt butter and add flour; cook, stirring constantly, 5 minutes or until golden. Stir in golden onion soup mix thoroughly blended with water. Bring to a boil, then simmer 15 minutes or until thickened. Stir in turkey, vegetables, 1 cup cheese and pepper. Turn into lightly greased 2-quart casserole; top with hot potatoes, then remaining ¼ cup cheese. Bake 30 minutes or until bubbling. *Makes about 8 servings*

MICROWAVE DIRECTIONS: In 2-quart casserole, heat butter at HIGH (100% power) 1 minute. Stir in flour and heat uncovered, stirring frequently, 2 minutes. Stir in golden onion soup mix thoroughly blended with water. Heat uncovered, stirring occasionally, 4 minutes or until thickened. Stir in turkey, vegetables, 1 cup cheese and pepper. Top with hot potatoes, then remaining ¼ cup cheese. Heat uncovered, turning casserole occasionally, 5 minutes or until bubbling. Let stand uncovered 5 minutes. For additional color, sprinkle, if desired, with paprika.

GOLDEN CHICKEN NORMANDY-STYLE

1 (2½- to 3-pound) chicken, cut-up
Salt and pepper
¼ cup flour
2 tablespoons butter or margarine
2 Golden Delicious apples (about 12 ounces), cored and sliced
¾ cup half-and-half
⅓ cup dry white wine
1 tablespoon lemon juice
2 tablespoons chopped fresh parsley

Season chicken with salt and pepper; coat in flour. In large skillet, melt butter. Brown chicken on all sides; remove from skillet. Add apples; brown lightly. Place chicken and apples in shallow 2½-quart baking dish. Bake at 350°F 20 minutes or until chicken is tender. Reserve 2 tablespoons pan drippings in skillet. Add half-and-half to skillet; cook and stir until thickened. Blend in wine and lemon juice. Add salt and pepper to taste; pour over chicken and apples. Sprinkle with chopped parsley. *Makes 4 servings*

Favorite recipe from ***Washington Apple Commission***

Turkey Cottage Pie

POTLUCK POCKETS

Nonstick cooking spray
½ pound lean ground turkey
¾ cup chopped onions
1 clove garlic, minced
½ cup sliced mushrooms
1 jar (14 ounces) spaghetti sauce
2½ cups all-purpose flour, divided
½ cup cornmeal
2 teaspoons baking powder
½ teaspoon dried oregano leaves
¼ cup margarine
1¼ cups KELLOGG'S® ALL-BRAN® cereal
1 cup skim milk
½ cup (2 ounces) shredded part-skim mozzarella cheese

In large skillet coated with nonstick cooking spray, cook turkey, onions and garlic over medium heat. Stir in mushrooms and spaghetti sauce. Cover; simmer an additional 20 minutes, stirring occasionally.

In medium bowl, stir together 2 cups flour, cornmeal, baking powder and oregano. With pastry blender, cut in margarine until mixture resembles coarse crumbs.

In small bowl, combine Kellogg's® All-Bran® cereal and milk. Let stand 3 minutes or until milk is absorbed. Add cereal mixture to flour mixture, stirring with fork until dough forms ball.

On lightly floured surface, knead in remaining flour until dough is smooth and elastic. Divide dough in half; roll to ⅛-inch thickness. With pastry cutter or small saucepan lid, cut dough into 6-inch rounds. Cover each round with 2 teaspoons cheese; top with ¼ cup turkey mixture. Fold rounds in half, pinching dough with fork to seal. Repeat with remaining dough. Place on baking sheet coated with nonstick cooking spray.

Bake at 350°F 20 minutes or until lightly browned. Serve warm. *Makes 12 servings*

FANCY CHICKEN PUFF PIE

4 tablespoons butter or margarine
¼ cup chopped shallots
¼ cup all-purpose flour
1 cup chicken stock or broth
¼ cup sherry
Salt to taste
⅛ teaspoon white pepper
Pinch ground nutmeg
¼ pound ham, cut into 2×¼-inch strips
3 cups cooked PERDUE® chicken, cut into 2¼-inch strips
1½ cups fresh asparagus pieces *or* 1 (10-ounce) package frozen asparagus pieces
1 cup (½ pint) heavy cream
Chilled pie crust for a 1-crust pie *or* 1 sheet frozen puff pastry
1 egg, beaten

In medium saucepan over medium-high heat, melt butter; cook and stir shallots lightly. Stir in flour; cook 3 minutes. Add broth and sherry. Heat to boiling, stirring constantly; season to taste with salt, pepper and nutmeg. Reduce heat to low and simmer 5 minutes. Stir in ham, chicken, asparagus and cream. Pour chicken mixture into ungreased 9-inch pie plate.

Preheat oven to 425°F. Cut 8-inch circle from crust. Cut hearts from extra dough with cookie cutter, if desired. Place circle on cookie sheet moistened with cold water. Pierce with fork, brush with egg and decorate with hearts; brush hearts with egg.

Bake crust and filled pie plate 10 minutes; reduce heat to 350°F and bake additional 10 to 15 minutes or until pastry is golden brown and filling is hot and set. With spatula, place pastry over hot filling and serve immediately.

Makes 4 servings

TASTY TURKEY ROLL

1 pound ground turkey
½ cup soft bread crumbs
¼ cup tomato juice
1 egg, beaten
2 cloves garlic, minced
¼ teaspoon dried oregano
¼ teaspoon pepper
¼ pound shaved turkey ham
1 cup grated mozzarella cheese
2 tablespoons chili sauce (optional)

In medium bowl, combine ground turkey, bread crumbs, juice, egg, garlic, oregano and pepper.

On rectangular 16×12-inch piece of waxed paper, shape turkey mixture into 12×9-inch rectangle. Place turkey ham over top of turkey mixture and sprinkle cheese over turkey ham. Roll turkey, jelly-roll style, using waxed paper to help make roll. Lightly press ends of roll to seal. Place turkey roll, seam side down, on baking sheet lightly coated with nonstick cooking spray.

Bake at 350°F 1 hour or until center of turkey roll reaches 160°F on meat thermometer and ground turkey is no longer pink.

To serve, drizzle 2 tablespoons chili sauce over top of roll, if desired, and cut into 12 equal pieces.

Makes 12 servings

Favorite recipe from ***National Turkey Federation***

GRILLED ROASTER WITH INTERNATIONAL BASTING SAUCES

1 PERDUE® Oven Stuffer Roaster (5 to 7 pounds)
Salt
Ground pepper
1 cup vegetable oil
⅓ cup red wine vinegar
1 teaspoon paprika

Remove and discard giblets from roaster; rinse bird and pat dry with paper towels. Sprinkle inside and out with salt and pepper; set aside. To prepare basting sauce, in small covered jar, combine oil, vinegar, paprika, 1 teaspoon salt and ½ teaspoon pepper. Shake well; set aside.

If using a gas grill, follow manufacturer's directions. If using a covered charcoal grill, prepare coals at least 30 minutes before grilling. Open all vents and place a drip pan at center in bottom of grill. Arrange 25 to 30 hot coals at either end of drip pan. For added smoky flavor, soak 1 cup mesquite, hickory, oak, apple or cherry wood chips in water and scatter onto hot coals.

When coals are covered with gray ash and are medium-hot (you can hold your hand over them 3 to 4 seconds), place roaster on grill over drip pan. Cover with grill lid and cook roaster about 2 hours until Bird Watcher thermometer pops up and juices run clear with no hint of pink when thigh is pierced. (Note: Smoking may cause meat to remain slightly pink.) Begin checking roaster for doneness after 1½ hours. If thermometer has popped, brush on basting sauce and grill 30 minutes longer. In small saucepan, bring remaining basting sauce to a boil; serve with carved roaster. Do not reuse sauce.

Makes 6 servings

SAUCE VARIATIONS:

Italian Roaster: Prepare basting sauce as directed, adding 2 cloves minced garlic, 1 cup ketchup, 1 teaspoon dried oregano and ½ teaspoon dried basil to mixture. Use only in last 10 minutes of grilling.

French Roaster: Prepare basting sauce as directed, adding ⅓ cup minced shallots, ⅓ cup Dijon-style mustard and 1 teaspoon crumbled dried tarragon to mixture.

German Roaster: Prepare basting sauce as directed, adding ½ cup beer, 2 tablespoons molasses and 2 tablespoons caraway seeds to mixture. Use only in last 10 minutes of grilling.

Chinese Roaster: Prepare basting sauce as directed, adding ⅓ cup soy sauce, 2 cloves minced garlic and 1 teaspoon ground ginger or 1 tablespoon grated fresh ginger root to mixture.

Grilled Roaster with International Basting Sauces

CREAMY TURKEY & BROCCOLI

- 1 package (6 ounces) stuffing mix,* plus ingredients to prepare mix
- 1 can (2.8 ounces) DURKEE® French Fried Onions
- 1 package (10 ounces) frozen broccoli spears, thawed and drained
- 1 package (1⅛ ounces) cheese sauce mix
- 1¼ cups milk
- ½ cup sour cream
- 2 cups (10 ounces) cubed cooked turkey or chicken

*Three cups leftover stuffing may be substituted for stuffing mix. If stuffing is dry, stir in water, 1 tablespoon at a time, until moist but not wet.

Preheat oven to 350°F. In medium saucepan, prepare stuffing mix according to package directions; stir in ½ can French Fried Onions. Spread stuffing over bottom of greased 9-inch round baking dish. Arrange broccoli spears over stuffing with florets around edge of dish. In medium saucepan, prepare cheese sauce mix according to package directions using 1¼ cups milk. Remove from heat; stir in sour cream and turkey. Pour turkey mixture over broccoli stalks. Bake, covered, at 350°F for 30 minutes or until heated through. Sprinkle remaining onions over turkey; bake, uncovered, 5 minutes or until onions are golden. *Makes 4 to 6 servings*

COUNTRY CAPTAIN CHICKEN AND RICE

- 1 to 2 tablespoons curry powder, as desired
- 1 teaspoon garlic powder
- 1 teaspoon salt (optional)
- ½ teaspoon dried thyme leaves
- ¼ teaspoon black pepper
- 6 chicken breast halves, boned and skinned
- 1 can (28 ounces) whole tomatoes
- 1 cup UNCLE BEN'S® CONVERTED® Brand Rice
- 1 cup golden raisins
- 1 tablespoon sugar
- ⅓ cup dry roasted peanuts (optional)

Combine curry powder, garlic powder, salt, thyme and pepper. Reserve 1 tablespoon. Sprinkle remaining spice mixture over chicken breasts; rub seasonings into surface of chicken. Drain tomatoes well, reserving liquid; chop tomatoes. If necessary, add enough water to tomato liquid to make 2 cups. Combine liquid, tomatoes, rice, raisins, sugar and reserved spice mixture in 10-inch skillet. Arrange chicken over rice mixture. Bring to a boil. Cover and simmer 20 minutes. Remove from heat. Let stand covered until all liquid is absorbed, about 5 minutes. Sprinkle with peanuts, if desired, before serving. *Makes 6 servings*

Creamy Turkey & Broccoli

DAIRYLAND CONFETTI CHICKEN

- **1 cup diced carrots**
- **¾ cup chopped onion**
- **½ cup diced celery**
- **¼ cup chicken broth**
- **1 can (10½ ounces) cream of chicken soup**
- **1 cup dairy sour cream**
- **3 cups cubed cooked chicken**
- **½ cup (4 ounces) sliced mushrooms**
- **1 teaspoon Worcestershire sauce**
- **1 teaspoon salt**
- **⅛ teaspoon pepper**
- **Confetti Topping (recipe follows)**

For casserole: In saucepan, combine carrots, onion, celery and chicken broth. Simmer 20 minutes. In 3-quart casserole, mix soup, sour cream, chicken cubes, mushrooms, Worcestershire sauce, salt and pepper. Add simmered vegetables and liquid; mix well. Drop tablespoons of Confetti Topping onto casserole and bake in 350°F oven for 40 to 45 minutes or until golden brown. Sprinkle with remaining ¼ cup cheese and return to oven until melted. Garnish as desired.

Makes 6 to 8 servings

Confetti Topping

- **1 cup sifted all-purpose flour**
- **2 teaspoons baking powder**
- **½ teaspoon salt**
- **2 eggs, slightly beaten**
- **½ cup milk**
- **1 tablespoon chopped green bell pepper**
- **1 tablespoon chopped pimiento**
- **1¼ cups (5 ounces) shredded Wisconsin Cheddar cheese, divided**

In mixing bowl, combine flour, baking powder and salt. Add eggs, milk, green pepper, pimiento and 1 cup of the cheese. Mix just until well blended.

Favorite recipe from ***Wisconsin Milk Marketing Board ©1995***

Dairyland Confetti Chicken

SEAFOOD

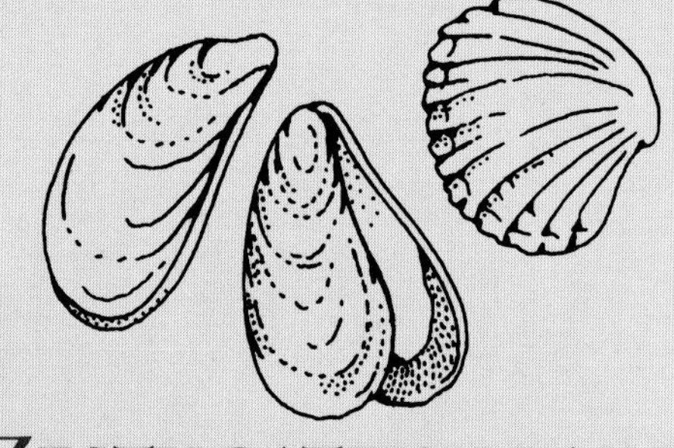

ZESTY CATFISH BAKE

6 (4- to 5-ounce) farm-raised catfish fillets
1 tablespoon butter
⅓ cup chopped onion
1 (8-ounce) package cream cheese, softened
¼ cup dry white wine
2 tablespoons shredded horseradish
1 tablespoon Dijon-style mustard
½ teaspoon salt
⅛ teaspoon pepper
4 strips bacon, cooked crisp, crumbled
2 tablespoons finely chopped fresh parsley

If frozen, thaw fish fillets; rinse and pat dry. Preheat oven to 350°F. Grease large baking dish. Arrange fillets in single layer in dish. Melt butter in skillet over medium-high heat. Add onion; cook and stir until softened. Combine cream cheese, wine, horseradish, mustard, salt and pepper in small bowl; stir in onion. Pour mixture over fish and top with crumbled bacon. Bake 30 minutes or until fish flakes easily when tested with fork. Garnish with parsley. *Makes 6 servings*

SEAFOOD

SHRIMP IN ANGEL HAIR PASTA CASSEROLE

- 1 tablespoon butter
- 2 eggs
- 1 cup half-and-half
- 1 cup plain yogurt
- ½ cup (4 ounces) shredded Swiss cheese
- ⅓ cup crumbled feta cheese
- ⅓ cup chopped fresh parsley
- ¼ cup chopped fresh basil *or* 1 teaspoon dried basil leaves, crushed
- 1 teaspoon dried oregano leaves, crushed
- 1 package (9 ounces) uncooked fresh angel hair pasta
- 1 jar (16 ounces) mild, thick and chunky salsa
- 1 pound medium shrimp, peeled and deveined
- ½ cup (4 ounces) shredded Monterey Jack cheese

With 1 tablespoon butter, grease 12×8-inch pan. Combine eggs, half-and-half, yogurt, Swiss cheese, feta cheese, parsley, basil and oregano in medium bowl; mix well. Spread ½ the pasta on bottom of prepared pan. Cover with salsa. Add ½ the shrimp. Cover with remaining pasta. Spread egg mixture over pasta and top with remaining shrimp. Sprinkle Monterey Jack cheese over top. Bake in preheated 350°F oven 30 minutes or until hot. Let stand 10 minutes. Garnish as desired.

Makes 6 servings

Favorite recipe from ***Southeast United Dairy Industry Association, Inc.***

LOUISIANA SEAFOOD BAKE

- ⅔ cup uncooked white rice
- 1 cup sliced celery
- 1 cup water
- 1 can (14½ ounces) whole tomatoes, undrained and cut up
- 1 can (8 ounces) tomato sauce
- 1 can (2.8 ounces) DURKEE® French Fried Onions
- 1 teaspoon REDHOT® Cayenne Pepper Sauce
- ½ teaspoon garlic powder
- ¼ teaspoon oregano leaves
- ¼ teaspoon thyme leaves
- ½ pound white fish (thawed if frozen), cut into 1-inch chunks
- 1 can (4 ounces) shrimp, drained
- ⅓ cup sliced pitted ripe olives
- ¼ cup (1 ounce) grated Parmesan cheese

Preheat oven to 375°F. In 1½-quart casserole, combine uncooked rice, celery, water, tomatoes with juice, tomato sauce, ½ can French Fried Onions and seasonings. Bake, covered, at 375°F for 20 minutes. Stir in fish, shrimp and olives. Bake, covered, 20 minutes or until heated through. Top with cheese and remaining onions; bake, uncovered, 3 minutes or until onions are golden.

Makes 4 servings

Shrimp in Angel Hair Pasta Casserole

SEAFOOD

TUNA WITH PEPPERCORNS ON A BED OF GREENS

- Salt
- 4 tuna steaks (about 1½ pounds)
- 2 teaspoons coarsely ground black pepper
- 1 large onion, thinly sliced
- 1 tablespoon butter or margarine
- ¼ cup dry white wine
- ½ pound fresh kale or spinach, cut into 1-inch strips
- ½ teaspoon sugar
- ¼ teaspoon black pepper
- 1 tablespoon olive oil
- Carrot strips (optional)

Preheat oven to 325°F. Lightly sprinkle salt over fish steaks, then press coarsely ground pepper onto both sides of steaks; set aside. Cook and stir onion in melted butter in large skillet over medium heat 5 minutes or until crisp-tender. Add wine; remove from heat. Spread onion mixture in 13×9-inch glass baking dish. Place fish on top. Bake 30 minutes or until fish flakes easily when tested with fork, turning fish over and basting with liquid halfway through baking time.

Cook and stir kale, sugar and black pepper in hot oil in medium skillet over medium-high heat 2 to 3 minutes or until tender. Place kale on plates; top with onion mixture, then fish. Place carrot strips over fish; garnish, if desired. *Makes 4 servings*

DILLED SALMON SUPPER

- 1 bottle (8 ounces) clam juice
- ½ cup dry vermouth
- ½ cup UNCLE BEN'S® CONVERTED® Brand Rice, uncooked
- 1 tablespoon lime juice
- 1 clove garlic, crushed
- 2 teaspoons chopped fresh dill *or* ½ teaspoon dried dill weed
- ⅛ teaspoon freshly ground black pepper
- 2 salmon steaks, ¾-inch thick* (about ¾ pound)
- ½ cup frozen peas, thawed
- ¼ cup plain low fat yogurt
- Paprika

*Haddock, halibut or red snapper fillets, ½- to ¾-inch thick, may be substituted.

Bring clam juice and vermouth to a boil in 10-inch skillet. Stir in rice, lime juice, garlic, dill and pepper. Arrange salmon steaks on top. Cover and simmer 20 minutes. Remove from heat. Gently stir peas into rice. Let stand covered until all liquid is absorbed, about 5 minutes. Top salmon with yogurt and sprinkle with paprika.

Makes 2 servings

Tuna with Peppercorns on a Bed of Greens

SEAFOOD

BAKED FISH WITH POTATOES AND ONIONS

1 pound baking potatoes, very thinly sliced
1 large onion, very thinly sliced
1 small red or green bell pepper, thinly sliced
Salt
Black pepper
½ teaspoon dried oregano leaves, crushed, divided
1 pound lean fish fillets, cut 1 inch thick
¼ cup butter or margarine
¼ cup all-purpose flour
2 cups milk
¾ cup (3 ounces) shredded Cheddar cheese

Preheat oven to 375°F.

Arrange ½ potatoes in buttered 3-quart casserole. Top with ½ onion and ½ bell pepper. Season with salt and black pepper. Sprinkle with ¼ teaspoon oregano. Arrange fish in 1 layer over vegetables. Arrange remaining potatoes, onion and bell pepper over fish. Season with salt, black pepper and remaining ¼ teaspoon oregano.

Melt butter in medium saucepan over medium heat. Stir in flour; cook until bubbly, stirring constantly. Gradually stir in milk. Cook until thickened, stirring constantly. Pour white sauce over casserole. Cover and bake at 375°F 40 minutes or until potatoes are tender. Sprinkle with cheese. Bake, uncovered, about 5 minutes more or until cheese is melted. *Makes 4 servings*

SEAFOOD PASTA SALAD

1 can (15¼ ounces) DOLE® Tropical Fruit Salad
6 ounces spiral pasta, hot, cooked
2 teaspoons toasted sesame oil
Fruity Dressing (recipe follows)
12 ounces cooked baby shrimp
2 cups (4 ounces) bean sprouts
1 cup snow peas
½ cup chopped DOLE® Celery
½ cup chopped DOLE® Red Bell Pepper
¼ cup DOLE® Chopped Dates
¼ cup dry roasted peanuts, coarsely chopped

- Drain tropical fruit salad; reserve ⅓ cup juice for dressing.
- Toss hot pasta with sesame oil. When cool, mix with Fruity Dressing.
- Add tropical fruit salad and remaining ingredients; toss to combine. *Makes 8 servings*

Fruity Dressing

¼ cup rice or white vinegar
2 tablespoons light soy sauce
2 tablespoons chopped fresh cilantro or parsley
1 teaspoon minced jalapeño or serrano chile

- Combine ⅓ cup juice, reserved from Tropical Fruit Salad, vinegar, soy sauce, cilantro and jalapeño; whisk to blend.

Baked Fish with Potatoes and Onions

SEAFOOD

COMPANY CRAB

- 1 pound blue crabmeat, fresh, frozen or pasteurized
- 1 can (15 ounces) artichoke hearts, drained
- 1 can (4 ounces) sliced mushrooms, drained
- 2 tablespoons butter or margarine
- 2½ tablespoons all-purpose flour
- ½ teaspoon salt
- ⅛ teaspoon ground red pepper
- 1 cup half-and-half
- 2 tablespoons dry sherry
- 2 tablespoons crushed corn flakes
- 1 tablespoon grated Parmesan cheese
- Paprika

Thaw crabmeat if frozen. Remove any pieces of shell or cartilage. Cut artichoke hearts in half. Place artichokes in well-greased, shallow 1½-quart casserole. Add crabmeat and mushrooms; cover and set aside.

Melt butter over medium heat in small saucepan. Stir in flour, salt and ground red pepper. Gradually stir in half-and-half. Continue cooking until sauce thickens, stirring constantly. Stir in sherry. Pour sauce over crabmeat. Combine corn flakes and cheese in small bowl; sprinkle over casserole. Sprinkle with paprika. Bake in preheated 450°F oven 12 to 15 minutes or until bubbly.

Makes 6 servings

Favorite recipe from **Florida Department of Agriculture and Consumer Sources**

OYSTER-ARTICHOKE PAN ROAST

- 1 (14-ounce) can artichoke hearts, drained and quartered
- 4 tablespoons butter or margarine
- 1 cup chopped green onions
- ½ cup chopped onion
- 1 clove garlic, minced
- 3 tablespoons flour
- 1 quart oysters with their liquor
- ½ cup chopped fresh parsley
- 1 tablespoon lemon juice
- 1 teaspoon Worcestershire sauce
- ¼ teaspoon TABASCO® pepper sauce
- ½ teaspoon salt
- 2 tablespoons butter or margarine
- 1 cup fresh bread crumbs

In small saucepan, place artichoke hearts in water. Bring to a simmer; keep warm.

In medium skillet, heat 4 tablespoons butter; cook and stir green onions, onion and garlic until tender. Sprinkle with flour. Cook and stir another 3 minutes to cook flour.

While vegetables are cooking, in medium saucepan poach oysters in their liquor (add water, if necessary) until edges curl and oysters plump up. Drain, reserving liquid.

Add 1 to 1½ cups oyster liquid to vegetables. Add parsley, lemon juice, Worcestershire sauce, TABASCO sauce and salt. Simmer until

SEAFOOD

thickened. Place oysters and artichokes in shallow casserole; cover with sauce. (Recipe may be prepared ahead of time up to this point.)

Heat oven to 350°F. In skillet, melt 2 tablespoons butter; stir in bread crumbs until well coated. Sprinkle over casserole. Bake at 350°F 15 to 20 minutes or until bread crumbs are browned and sauce is bubbly. *Makes 4 servings*

CRISPY CATFISH NUGGETS WITH CREOLE SAUCE

4½ cups KELLOGG'S® CORN FLAKES® cereal, crushed to 2 cups
½ teaspoon paprika
½ teaspoon onion powder
1 cup skim milk
1 egg, beaten
1 pound catfish nuggets (about 36 nuggets)
Nonstick cooking spray
1 clove garlic, minced
1 tablespoon olive oil
½ cup chopped onion
½ cup chopped green pepper
¼ cup chopped celery
1 tablespoon sugar
¼ teaspoon red pepper flakes
1 can (6 ounces) tomato paste
½ cup water

1. Stir together crushed Kellogg's® Corn Flakes®, paprika and onion powder in shallow dish or pan. Set aside.

2. Combine milk and egg in second shallow dish or pan. Dip catfish nuggets into egg mixture. Coat with cereal mixture. Place on baking sheet coated with cooking spray.

3. Bake at 350°F about 20 minutes. Serve warm with Creole Sauce.

4. **To make Creole Sauce:** in saucepan, cook garlic in oil over medium heat until browned. Add onion, green pepper, celery, sugar and red pepper flakes. Cook until vegetables are tender. Stir in tomato paste and water. Cover; simmer 15 minutes. Serve with catfish nuggets.

Makes 3 dozen nuggets, 1⅔ cups sauce

QUICK AND EASY TUNA RICE WITH PEAS

1 package (10 ounces) green peas
1¼ cups water
1 can (11 ounces) condensed Cheddar cheese soup
1 can (12½ ounces) tuna, drained and flaked
1 chicken bouillon cube
1½ cups MINUTE® Rice

• Bring peas, water, soup, tuna and bouillon cube to a full boil in medium saucepan. Stir in rice. Cover; remove from heat. Let stand 5 minutes. Fluff with fork. *Makes 4 servings*

SEAFOOD

HERB-BAKED FISH & RICE

- 1½ cups hot chicken bouillon
- ½ cup uncooked white rice (not instant)
- ¼ teaspoon Italian seasoning
- ¼ teaspoon garlic powder
- 1 package (10 ounces) frozen chopped broccoli, thawed and drained
- 1 can (2.8 ounces) DURKEE® French Fried Onions
- 1 tablespoon grated Parmesan cheese
- 1 pound unbreaded fish fillets (thawed if frozen)
- Paprika
- ½ cup (2 ounces) shredded Cheddar cheese

Preheat oven to 375°F. In 12×8-inch baking dish, combine hot bouillon, uncooked rice and seasonings. Bake, covered, at 375°F for 10 minutes. Top with broccoli, ½ can French Fried Onions and Parmesan cheese. Place fish fillets diagonally down center of dish; sprinkle fish lightly with paprika. Bake, covered, at 375°F 20 to 25 minutes or until fish flakes easily with fork. Stir rice. Top fish with Cheddar cheese and remaining onions; bake, uncovered, 3 minutes or until onions are golden. *Makes 3 to 4 servings*

OLD-FASHIONED TUNA NOODLE CASSEROLE

- ¼ cup plain dry bread crumbs
- 3 tablespoons butter or margarine, melted and divided
- 1 tablespoon finely chopped parsley
- ½ cup chopped onion
- ½ cup chopped celery
- 1 cup water
- 1 cup milk
- 1 package LIPTON® Noodles & Sauce–Butter
- 2 cans (6½ ounces each) tuna, drained and flaked

In small bowl, thoroughly combine bread crumbs, 1 tablespoon butter and parsley; set aside.

In medium saucepan, melt remaining 2 tablespoons butter. Cook onion and celery over medium heat, stirring occasionally, 2 minutes or until onion is tender. Add water and milk; bring to a boil. Stir in Noodles & Butter Sauce. Continue boiling over medium heat, stirring occasionally, 8 minutes or until noodles are tender. Stir in tuna. Turn into greased 1-quart casserole, then top with bread crumb mixture. Broil until bread crumbs are golden. *Makes about 4 servings*

Herb-Baked Fish & Rice

SEAFOOD

Chesapeake Crab Strata

4 tablespoons butter or margarine
4 cups unseasoned croutons
2 cups shredded Cheddar cheese
2 cups milk
8 eggs, beaten
½ teaspoon dry mustard
½ teaspoon seafood seasoning
Salt and black pepper to taste
1 pound crabmeat, picked over to remove any shells

Preheat oven to 325°F. Place butter in 11×7×1½-inch baking dish. Heat in oven until melted, tilting to coat dish. Remove dish from oven; spread croutons over melted butter. Top with cheese; set aside.

Combine milk, eggs, dry mustard, seafood seasoning, salt and black pepper; mix well. Pour egg mixture over cheese in dish and sprinkle crabmeat on top. Bake for 50 minutes or until mixture is set. Remove from oven and let stand for about 10 minutes. Garnish with pepper rings, if desired. *Makes 6 to 8 servings*

Shrimp in Cajun Red Gravy

1 tablespoon plus 2 teaspoons Chef Paul Prudhomme's SEAFOOD MAGIC®, in all
1 pound medium to large shelled, deveined shrimp
2 tablespoons unsalted butter
3 tablespoons olive oil
1 cup finely chopped onion
½ cup finely chopped green bell pepper
¼ cup finely chopped celery
2 bay leaves
1 tablespoon minced fresh garlic
2 cups canned crushed tomatoes
1 tablespoon dark brown sugar
1½ cups water
Hot cooked rice or pasta

Add 2 teaspoons of the Seafood Magic® to shrimp and mix well. Reserve. Melt butter in 10-inch skillet over high heat. Add olive oil and heat 1½ minutes or until mixture comes to a hard sizzle. Stir in onion, bell pepper, celery, remaining 1 tablespoon Seafood Magic® and bay leaves. Cook, stirring occasionally, 5 to 6 minutes or until vegetables begin to soften. Add garlic and tomatoes; cook, stirring occasionally, about 8 minutes. Stir in brown sugar and water. Cook, stirring occasionally, 4 minutes or until mixture boils rapidly. Add shrimp and stir well. Cook 2 minutes or just until shrimp are plump and pink. Turn heat off. Cover skillet; let stand 5 minutes. Serve over hot cooked rice or pasta.

Makes 4 servings

Chesapeake Crab Strata

DELIGHTFUL DESSERTS

PEANUT CHOCOLATE SURPRISE PIE

8 tablespoons (1 stick) butter, melted
1 cup granulated sugar
2 eggs
½ cup all-purpose flour
½ cup chopped peanuts
½ cup chopped walnuts
½ cup semisweet chocolate chips
¼ cup bourbon
1 teaspoon vanilla extract
1 (9-inch) unbaked deep-dish pie shell
Whipped cream, for garnish
Chocolate shavings, for garnish

Preheat oven to 350°F. Cream butter and sugar in large bowl. Add eggs and beat until well mixed. Gradually add flour, then stir in nuts, chips, bourbon and vanilla. Spread mixture evenly in unbaked pie shell. Bake 40 minutes. Cool pie on wire rack; decorate with whipped cream and chocolate shavings. *Makes one 9-inch pie*

BERRY COBBLER

1 pint fresh raspberries (2½ cups)*
1 pint fresh blueberries or strawberries, sliced (2½ cups)*
⅓ cup sugar
2 tablespoons cornstarch
1 cup all-purpose flour
1 tablespoon sugar
1½ teaspoons baking powder
¼ teaspoon salt
½ cup milk
⅓ cup butter or margarine, melted
¼ teaspoon ground nutmeg

*One (16-ounce) bag frozen raspberries and one (16-ounce) bag frozen blueberries or strawberries may be substituted for fresh berries. Thaw berries, reserving juices. Increase cornstarch to 3 tablespoons.

Preheat oven to 375°F. Combine berries, 1/3 cup sugar and cornstarch in medium bowl; toss lightly to coat. Spoon into 1½-quart or 8-inch square baking dish. Combine flour, 1 tablespoon sugar, baking powder and salt in medium bowl. Add milk and butter; mix just until dry ingredients are moistened. Drop six heaping tablespoonfuls of batter evenly over berries; sprinkle with nutmeg. Bake 25 minutes or until topping is golden brown and fruit is bubbly. Cool on wire rack. Serve warm or at room temperature. *Makes 6 servings*

PICKLED PEACHES

6 pounds firm-ripe peaches, peeled, pitted and halved
6¾ cups sugar
3½ cups white vinegar (labeled 5% acidity)
4 (2½-inch) cinnamon sticks
1 tablespoon whole cloves
1 tablespoon ground ginger

Combine sugar and vinegar in a 6- to 8-quart saucepan. Bring to a boil; continue boiling 5 minutes. Tie spices in spice bag or cheesecloth. Add spice bag and peaches to syrup. Simmer 5 to 10 minutes or until peaches are cooked but not too soft, stirring peaches gently to cook all sides. Cover and let stand in cool place for 12 to 18 hours, stirring peaches 2 or 3 times.

Bring peaches and syrup to a boil. Remove from heat and remove spices. Skim off foam, if necessary. Immediately fill hot pint or quart jars with mixture, leaving 1/2-inch headspace.

Carefully run nonmetallic utensil down inside of jars to remove trapped air bubbles. Wipe jar tops and threads clean. Place hot lids on jars and screw bands on firmly. Process in Boiling Water Canner (page 36) 25 minutes for quarts or 20 minutes for pints. *Makes about 2 quarts or 4 to 5 pints*

Favorite recipe from ***Kerr Group, Inc.®***

Berry Cobbler

MARVELOUS MACAROONS

1 can (8 ounces) DOLE® Crushed Pineapple in Juice
1 can (14 ounces) sweetened condensed milk
1 package (7 ounces) flaked coconut
½ cup DOLE® Chopped Almonds, toasted
½ cup margarine, melted
Grated peel from 1 DOLE® Lemon
¼ teaspoon almond extract
1 cup all-purpose flour
1 teaspoon baking powder

- Drain pineapple well; reserve juice for beverage.
- Combine drained pineapple, sweetened condensed milk, coconut, almonds, margarine, 1 teaspoon lemon peel and almond extract.
- Combine flour and baking powder. Beat into pineapple mixture until blended.
- Drop by heaping tablespoonfuls, 1 inch apart, onto greased cookie sheets. Bake in 350°F oven 13 to 15 minutes. Remove to wire racks to cool. Store in refrigerator. *Makes 3½ dozen cookies*

APRICOT-PEAR STRUDEL

2 sheets frozen puff pastry
1 (17-ounce) can California apricots, drained and sliced
1 (16-ounce) can pears, drained and cut into chunks
½ cup blanched slivered almonds
¼ cup packed light brown sugar
½ teaspoon ground cinnamon
½ teaspoon nutmeg
1 egg, beaten with 1 teaspoon water

Thaw pastry 20 minutes; unfold and place second sheet directly on top of first sheet. Roll on lightly floured surface to 14×10-inch rectangle. In large bowl, combine apricots, pears, almonds, brown sugar, cinnamon and nutmeg. Spoon fruit filling lengthwise down center third of pastry. Brush edges with egg-water mixture. Fold left side of pastry over filling; fold right side of pastry over to enclose filling completely. Pinch edges to seal. Roll strudel over onto ungreased baking sheet; seal edges by pressing with fork. Brush top with egg-water mixture; refrigerate, covered, 30 minutes or overnight. Preheat oven to 425°F. With sharp knife, lightly score top of strudel. Bake 25 to 30 minutes or until puffed and golden brown. Cool on wire rack for 30 minutes. *Makes 8 servings*

Favorite recipe from ***California Apricot Advisory Board***

OLD-FASHIONED UPSIDE-DOWN CAKE

- **⅔ cup margarine, divided**
- **⅔ cup brown sugar, packed**
- **1 can (20 ounces) DOLE® Pineapple Slices in Syrup or Juice**
- **10 maraschino cherries**
- **¾ cup granulated sugar, divided**
- **2 eggs, separated**
- **1 teaspoon grated lemon peel**
- **1 teaspoon lemon juice**
- **1 teaspoon vanilla extract**
- **1½ cups all-purpose flour**
- **1¾ teaspoons baking powder**
- **¼ teaspoon salt**
- **½ cup dairy sour cream**

• Melt ⅓ cup margarine in 10-inch cast iron skillet. Remove from heat. Add brown sugar and stir until blended.

• Drain pineapple well; reserve 2 tablespoons syrup. Arrange pineapple in sugar mixture. Place cherry in center of each slice.

• Beat remaining ⅓ cup margarine with ½ cup granulated sugar until light and fluffy. Beat in egg yolks, lemon peel, lemon juice and vanilla.

• Combine flour, baking powder and salt. Blend into creamed mixture alternately with sour cream and reserved 2 tablespoons pineapple syrup.

• Beat egg whites to soft peaks. Gradually beat in remaining ¼ cup granulated sugar until stiff peaks form. Fold into batter. Pour over pineapple in skillet. Bake in 350°F oven about 35 minutes or until wooden pick inserted in center comes out clean. Let stand 10 minutes, then invert onto serving plate. Serve warm or cold.

Makes 8 servings

BLACK BOTTOM BANANA CREAM PIE

- **2 tablespoons BLUE BONNET® 75% Vegetable Oil Spread**
- **4 (1-ounce) squares semisweet chocolate**
- **1 NILLA® Pie Crust**
- **2 small bananas, sliced**
- **1 (3⅜-ounce) package ROYAL® Instant Vanilla Pudding & Pie Filling**
- **2 cups cold milk**
- **Whipped topping, for garnish**

In small saucepan, over low heat, melt spread and chocolate, stirring until smooth. Spread evenly over bottom of crust. Arrange banana slices over chocolate; set aside.

Prepare pudding according to package directions for pie using milk; pour over bananas. Chill at least 1 hour. Garnish with whipped topping.

Makes 8 servings

FRESH LEMON MERINGUE PIE

1½ cups sugar
¼ cup plus 2 tablespoons cornstarch
½ teaspoon salt
½ cup cold water
½ cup fresh squeezed lemon juice
3 egg yolks, well beaten
2 tablespoons butter or margarine
1½ cups boiling water
Grated peel of ½ SUNKIST® Lemon
2 to 3 drops yellow food coloring (optional)
1 (9-inch) baked pie crust
Three-Egg Meringue (recipe follows)

In large saucepan, combine sugar, cornstarch and salt. Gradually blend in cold water and lemon juice. Stir in egg yolks. Add butter and boiling water. Bring to a boil over medium-high heat, stirring constantly. Reduce heat to medium and boil 1 minute. Remove from heat; stir in lemon peel and food coloring. Pour into baked pie crust. Top with Three-Egg Meringue, sealing well at edges. Bake at 350°F 12 to 15 minutes. Cool 2 hours before serving. *Makes 6 servings*

Three-Egg Meringue

3 egg whites
¼ teaspoon cream of tartar
6 tablespoons sugar

In large bowl, with electric mixer, beat egg whites with cream of tartar until foamy. Gradually add sugar and beat until stiff peaks form.

PEACH COBBLER

4 cups sliced peeled peaches *or* 2 (29-ounce) cans sliced peaches, drained
1 cup fresh or frozen blueberries (optional)
⅔ cup all-purpose flour, divided
⅓ cup sugar, divided
2 tablespoons lemon juice
⅓ cup BLUE BONNET® 75% Vegetable Oil Spread, softened, divided
20 NILLA® Wafers, finely rolled (about ¾ cups crumbs)
2 tablespoons water

In large bowl, toss peaches and blueberries with 2 tablespoons flour, 3 tablespoons sugar and lemon juice. Place in greased 8×8×2-inch baking dish; dot with 1 tablespoon spread.

In medium bowl, combine wafer crumbs with remaining flour and sugar; cut in remaining spread until mixture resembles coarse crumbs. Stir in water until mixture holds together; shape into ball. Roll dough out between 2 sheets of lightly floured waxed paper to 7½-inch circle. Remove 1 sheet of waxed paper. Cut 1-inch circle out of center of dough. Invert dough over fruit mixture; peel off paper. Sprinkle with additional sugar if desired.

Bake at 400°F for 35 to 40 minutes or until pastry is browned. Cool slightly before serving.

Makes 8 servings

Fresh Lemon Meringue Pie

ORANGE AMBROSIA CAKE ROLL

CAKE

- **1 cup cake flour**
- **1 teaspoon baking powder**
- **¼ teaspoon salt**
- **3 eggs**
- **1 cup sugar**
- **⅓ cup fresh squeezed orange juice**
- **Grated peel of ½ SUNKIST® Orange**
- **Orange slices (optional)**
- **Maraschino cherries (optional)**

ORANGE FILLING AND GLAZE

- **¾ cup sugar**
- **1 tablespoon cornstarch**
- **1 cup fresh squeezed orange juice**
- **4 egg yolks, beaten**
- **1 cup heavy cream or whipping cream, whipped**
- **Grated peel of 1 SUNKIST® Orange**
- **¼ cup shredded or flaked coconut**

To make Cake: Line 15½×10½×1-inch jellyroll pan with greased aluminum foil. In medium bowl, combine cake flour, baking powder and salt. In large bowl, with electric mixer, beat eggs well. Gradually add sugar and orange juice, beating until well blended. Gradually add dry ingredients, beating just until smooth. Stir in orange peel. Pour batter into prepared pan. Bake at 375°F 13 to 15 minutes. Cool 5 minutes. Invert cake onto large, waxed paper-lined cookie sheet; carefully remove foil. Roll up cake with waxed paper starting at narrow end; cool completely on wire rack.

To make Orange Filling and Glaze: In saucepan, combine sugar and cornstarch. Gradually blend in orange juice and beaten egg yolks. Bring to a boil over medium heat, stirring until thickened. Cool thoroughly. Reserve ½ cup cooled filling for glaze. Gently fold whipped cream and orange peel into remaining 1 cup filling.

To assemble cake roll: Unroll cake and spread with filling. Reroll without waxed paper and place on serving platter. Spread top with reserved glaze and sprinkle with coconut. Chill for at least 1 hour before serving. Garnish with orange twists and well-drained maraschino cherries with stems, if desired.

Makes 8 to 12 servings

Left to right: Orange Ambrosia Cake Roll; Karen Ann's Lemon Cake (page 114)

Sunkist
Sunkist

KAREN ANN'S LEMON CAKE

2 cups all-purpose flour
1½ teaspoons baking powder
½ teaspoon baking soda
¼ teaspoon salt
⅔ cup butter or margarine, softened
1¼ cups granulated sugar
3 eggs, separated
¾ cup sour cream
Grated peel of 1 SUNKIST® Lemon
Lemony Frosting (recipe follows)

Line two 8-inch round cake pans with waxed paper. Preheat oven to 350°F. In medium bowl, combine flour, baking powder, baking soda and salt. In large bowl, with electric mixer, cream together butter and sugar. Beat in egg yolks one at a time; continue beating until light in color. Add dry ingredients to creamed mixture alternately with sour cream, beating just until smooth. With clean beaters, beat egg whites until soft peaks form. Gently fold egg whites and lemon peel into batter. Pour into pans. Bake 30 to 35 minutes or until wooden pick inserted in center comes out clean. Cool 10 minutes. Remove from pans; peel off waxed paper. Cool on wire racks. Fill and frost with Lemony Frosting. *Makes 12 servings*

Lemony Frosting

½ cup butter or margarine, softened
3 cups confectioners' sugar, divided
Grated peel of ½ SUNKIST® Lemon
2 tablespoons fresh squeezed lemon juice

In medium bowl, cream together butter and 1 cup confectioners' sugar. Add lemon peel, lemon juice and remaining 2 cups sugar; beat until smooth.
Makes about 1¾ cups frosting

APPLE-BUTTERMILK PIE

2 medium-size Granny Smith apples
3 eggs
1½ cups sugar, divided
1 cup buttermilk
⅓ cup margarine or butter, melted
2 tablespoons all-purpose flour
2 teaspoons vanilla extract
1 tablespoon ground cinnamon, divided
2 teaspoons ground nutmeg, divided
1 (9-inch) unbaked pie shell

Preheat oven to 350°F. Peel and core apples; cut into small chunks. Place apples in bowl; cover with cold water and set aside. Beat eggs briefly at low speed of electric mixer until mixed. Reserve 1 tablespoon sugar. Add remaining sugar, buttermilk, margarine, flour, vanilla, 2 teaspoons cinnamon and 1½ teaspoons nutmeg; mix at low speed until well blended. Drain apples thoroughly and place in unbaked pie shell. Pour buttermilk mixture over apples. Combine reserved 1 teaspoon sugar, 1 teaspoon cinnamon and ½ teaspoon nutmeg; sprinkle over top. Bake 50 to 60 minutes. Serve warm or at room temperature for the best flavor. Store in refrigerator. *Makes one 9-inch pie*

Apple-Buttermilk Pie

GINGERBREAD COOKIES

- ½ cup FLEISCHMANN'S® Margarine, softened
- ¾ cup firmly packed light brown sugar
- ¾ cup light molasses
- ¼ cup EGG BEATERS® 99% Real Egg Product
- 4½ cups all-purpose flour
- 2 teaspoons baking soda
- 2 teaspoons ground cinnamon
- 2 teaspoons ground ginger
- ½ teaspoon ground cloves
- ½ teaspoon ground nutmeg
- Frosting and assorted candies for decorating

Cream margarine and sugar. Beat in molasses and egg product. Combine flour, baking soda and spices. Stir into margarine mixture to make stiff dough. Divide dough in half; wrap and chill for several hours or overnight.

Roll small amount of dough out onto well greased and floured baking sheets. Cut with desired 4-inch cookie cutters. Remove scraps and reroll. Bake at 350°F for 8 to 10 minutes or just until set and lightly brown. Cool completely on wire racks. Decorate cookies with frosting and assorted candies.

Makes 4 dozen cookies

STRAWBERRY PRESERVES

- 1½ quarts (approximately 6 cups) stemmed, firm-ripe strawberries
- 5 cups sugar
- ⅓ cup bottled lemon juice

Combine strawberries and sugar in a 6- to 8-quart saucepan. Cover and let stand 3 to 4 hours. Bring to a boil over medium heat, stirring occasionally, being careful to not break up fruit. Cook until sugar dissolves. Add lemon juice. Bring to a boil and cook to jelly stage (220°F), approximately 30 minutes, stirring frequently. Pour into a shallow pan. Let stand, uncovered, in a cool place for 12 to 24 hours.

Return to a saucepan. Bring fruit and syrup to a boil. Remove from heat and skim off foam, if necessary. Immediately fill hot, sterilized half-pint jars with mixture, leaving ¼-inch headspace. Carefully run a nonmetallic utensil down inside of jars to remove trapped air bubbles. Wipe jar tops and threads clean. Place hot lids and screw bands on firmly. Process in Boiling Water Canner (see page 36) for 5 minutes.

Makes approximately 4 half-pints

Favorite recipe from ***Kerr Group, Inc.®***

CHOCOLATE BANANA SPLIT PIE

- **1 cup sugar**
- **⅓ cup cocoa**
- **¼ cup cornstarch**
- **2½ tablespoons all-purpose flour**
- **¼ teaspoon salt**
- **2½ cups milk**
- **2 egg yolks, slightly beaten**
- **2 tablespoons margarine**
- **1 teaspoon vanilla extract**
- **3 firm, medium DOLE® Bananas, peeled**
- **Crumb-Nut Crust (recipe follows)**
- **Frozen whipped topping, thawed**
- **DOLE® Chopped Almonds or peanuts**
- **Maraschino cherries**

• **MICROWAVE DIRECTIONS:** In 2-quart microwave bowl, combine sugar, cocoa, cornstarch, flour and salt. Blend in milk and egg yolks. Microwave on HIGH (100% power) 6 to 8 minutes, whisking every 2 minutes or until mixture begins to boil. Microwave additional minute until thickened. Blend in margarine and vanilla. Press plastic wrap onto surface; cool.

• Slice 2 bananas; arrange over bottom of crust. Pour filling over bananas; press plastic wrap onto filling. Refrigerate 4 to 5 hours.

• Remove plastic wrap. Top pie with dollops of whipped topping. Slice remaining banana. Garnish with almonds, remaining sliced banana and cherries. *Makes 8 servings*

Crumb-Nut Crust

- **6 tablespoons margarine**
- **1¼ cups graham cracker crumbs**
- **¼ cup DOLE® Chopped Almonds**

In small microwavable bowl, microwave margarine 45 seconds or until melted. Stir in graham cracker crumbs and almonds.

Press on bottom and up sides of greased microwave 9-inch pie plate. Microwave 1½ to 2 minutes. Cool. *Makes one 9-inch pie crust*

GRANNY SMITH CRISP

- **5 cups peeled, cored and sliced Granny Smith apples**
- **½ cup sugar**
- **1 teaspoon ground cinnamon**
- **Streusel Topping (recipe follows)**

Heat oven to 350°F. In large bowl, toss apples with sugar and cinnamon; spread apple mixture in 11×8-inch baking pan. Prepare Streusel Topping; spread evenly over apples. Bake 35 to 40 minutes or until apples are tender. *Makes 6 servings*

Streusel Topping: In medium bowl, combine ¾ cup all-purpose flour, ¼ cup packed brown sugar and ¼ cup granulated sugar. With pastry blender or 2 knives, cut in ½ cup (1 stick) butter until crumbly mixture is formed. Stir in ½ cup quick rolled oats.

Favorite recipe from ***Washington Apple Commission***

Chocolate Caramel Pecan Bars

- **2 cups butter, softened and divided**
- **½ cup granulated sugar, divided**
- **1 egg**
- **2¾ cups all-purpose flour**
- **⅔ cup packed light brown sugar**
- **¼ cup light corn syrup**
- **2½ cups coarsely chopped pecans**
- **1 cup semisweet chocolate chips**

Preheat oven to 375°F. Grease 15×10-inch jelly-roll pan. Beat 1 cup butter and granulated sugar in large bowl until light and fluffy. Beat in egg. Add flour; beat until well blended. Pat dough in prepared pan. Bake 20 minutes or until light golden brown.

For topping, combine remaining 1 cup butter, brown sugar and corn syrup in medium, heavy saucepan. Cook over medium heat until mixture boils, stirring frequently. Boil gently 2 minutes without stirring. Quickly stir in pecans and spread topping evenly over base. Return bars to oven and bake 20 minutes or until dark golden brown and bubbling.

Immediately sprinkle chocolate chips evenly over caramel topping. Gently press chips into caramel with spatula. Loosen caramel from edges of pan. Place pan on wire rack to cool. Cut into 3 ×1½-inch bars. Store tightly covered at room temperature. *Makes 40 bars*

Apple Sunshine Dessert

- **4 to 5 Winesap apples**
- **½ cup sugar**
- **½ cup nonfat dry milk**
- **⅔ cup uncooked quick-cooking oats**
- **¼ cup flaked coconut**
- **¼ cup chopped almonds**
- **¼ cup packed brown sugar**
- **2 tablespoons wheat germ**
- **2 tablespoons sesame seeds**
- **½ teaspoon ground cinnamon**
- **¼ teaspoon ground nutmeg**
- **¼ cup butter or margarine, melted**
- **Dairy sour cream or yogurt**

Peel, core and slice apples to measure 4 cups; reserve 8 or 9 slices. Toss remaining apples with sugar and dry milk; place in 1½ quart baking dish. Arrange reserved slices on top. Cover with foil; bake at 375°F 15 minutes. Combine remaining ingredients except sour cream or yogurt; mix well. Uncover apples and sprinkle with oat mixture. Bake, uncovered, 18 to 20 minutes or until topping is golden brown. Serve warm topped with sour cream or yogurt. *Makes 6 servings*

Favorite recipe from ***Washington Apple Commission***

Chocolate Caramel Pecan Bars

PRALINE PUMPKIN TART

- **1¼ cups all-purpose flour**
- **1 tablespoon granulated sugar**
- **¾ teaspoon salt, divided**
- **¼ cup vegetable shortening**
- **¼ cup butter or margarine**
- **2 to 3 tablespoons cold water**
- **1 can (16 ounces) solid-pack pumpkin**
- **1 can (13 ounces) evaporated milk**
- **2 eggs**
- **⅔ cup packed brown sugar**
- **1 teaspoon ground cinnamon**
- **½ teaspoon ground ginger**
- **¼ teaspoon ground cloves**
- **Praline Topping (recipe follows)**
- **Sweetened Whipped Cream (recipe follows)**
- **Additional ground cinnamon and pecan halves for garnish**

Combine flour, granulated sugar and ¼ teaspoon salt in large bowl. Cut in shortening and butter with pastry blender until mixture forms pea-sized pieces. Sprinkle water, 1 tablespoon at a time, over flour mixture, tossing with fork after each addition until mixture holds together. Form into a ball. Wrap in plastic wrap; refrigerate 1 hour or until chilled.

Roll out dough on lightly floured surface 1 inch larger than inverted 10-inch tart pan with removable bottom. Place dough in tart pan; cut dough even with edge. Cover; refrigerate 30 minutes.

Preheat oven to 400°F. Prick crust with fork. Bake 15 minutes or until set. Place pan on wire rack to cool completely.

Preheat oven to 400°F. Beat pumpkin, milk, eggs, brown sugar, 1 teaspoon cinnamon, remaining ½ teaspoon salt, ginger and cloves in large bowl until blended. Pour into cooled tart crust. Bake 35 minutes.

Meanwhile, prepare Praline Topping and Sweetened Whipped Cream. Sprinkle topping over center of tart, leaving 1½-inch rim around edge. Bake 15 minutes or until knife inserted 1 inch from center comes out clean. Cool completely on wire rack. Remove side of pan. Pipe edge of tart with Sweetened Whipped Cream; sprinkle with additional cinnamon and garnish with pecans. *Makes 8 servings*

Praline Topping

- **⅓ cup *each* packed brown sugar, chopped pecans and uncooked quick-cooking oats**
- **1 tablespoon butter or margarine, softened**

Place sugar, pecans and oats in small bowl. Cut in butter with pastry blender until crumbs form.

Sweetened Whipped Cream

- **1 cup whipping cream**
- **2 tablespoons powdered sugar**
- **½ teaspoon vanilla**

Place all ingredients in chilled bowl. Beat until soft peaks form. *Do not overbeat.* Refrigerate.

Praline Pumpkin Tart

CALIFORNIA APRICOT-CHERRY CORNMEAL COBBLER

- **2 cups sliced fresh California apricots (about 1 pound)**
- **⅓ cup granulated sugar**
- **2 cups pitted fresh California cherries (about 8 ounces)**
- **1 tablespoon all-purpose flour**

BISCUIT DOUGH

- **1 cup all-purpose flour**
- **½ cup yellow cornmeal**
- **1½ tablespoons plus 1 teaspoon granulated sugar**
- **2 teaspoons baking powder**
- **¼ teaspoon salt**
- **½ teaspoon grated orange peel**
- **5 tablespoons unsalted butter, chilled**
- **¾ cup low fat milk**

Preheat oven to 375°F. In bowl, mix apricots and ⅓ cup sugar. In separate bowl, mix cherries and 1 tablespoon flour. For Biscuit Dough, in bowl, mix flour, cornmeal, 1½ tablespoons sugar, baking powder and salt; add orange peel. Cut in butter until mixture resembles coarse meal. Add milk; combine until just moistened. Combine fruit in 1½-quart baking dish; spoon batter over top. Sprinkle with remaining 1 teaspoon sugar. Bake 25 to 30 minutes or until golden brown. Cool slightly.

Makes 8 servings

Favorite recipe from ***California Apricot Advisory Board***

GOLDEN APPLE CHEESECAKE

- **Pastry (recipe follows)**
- **4 to 5 Golden Delicious apples**
- **1 package (8 ounces) cream cheese, softened**
- **Sugar**
- **1 egg**
- **½ teaspoon grated lemon peel**
- **¼ teaspoon vanilla**
- **⅛ teaspoon salt**
- **½ teaspoon ground cinnamon**
- **¼ cup sliced almonds**

Prepare pastry; set aside. Peel, core and slice apples to measure 4 cups. Place apples in shallow pan; cover with foil. Bake at 400°F 15 minutes. Meanwhile, beat cream cheese with ¼ cup sugar. Beat in egg, lemon peel, vanilla and salt until smooth; spoon into partially baked pastry. Arrange warm, partially cooked apple slices on top. Combine ⅓ cup sugar and cinnamon; sprinkle over apples. Top with almonds. Bake at 400°F 35 to 40 minutes or until crust is brown and apples are tender. Cool before cutting.

Makes 8 to 10 servings

Pastry: Combine ⅓ cup sugar, 6 tablespoons butter, ¼ teaspoon vanilla and ⅛ teaspoon salt. Blend in 1 cup flour. Pat onto bottom and 1¼ inches up sides of lightly greased 9-inch springform pan. Bake at 400°F 10 minutes. Cool.

Favorite recipe from ***Washington Apple Commission***

California Apricot-Cherry Cornmeal Cobbler

—Acknowledgments—

The publishers would like to thank the companies and organizations listed below for the use of their recipes and photographs in this publication.

American Lamb Council
Armour Swift-Eckrich
Borden Kitchens, Borden, Inc.
California Apricot Advisory Board
Chef Paul Prudhomme's Magic Seasoning Blends™
Dole Food Company, Inc.
Florida Department of Agriculture and Consumer Services
Florida Department of Citrus
Heinz U.S.A.
The HVR Company
Kellogg Company
Kerr Group, Inc.®
The Kingsford Products Company
Kraft General Foods, Inc.
Lawry's® Foods, Inc.
Thomas J. Lipton Co.
Louis Rich Company
McIlhenny Company
Nabisco Foods Group
National Broiler Council
National Live Stock & Meat Board
National Pork Producers Council
National Turkey Federation
North Dakota Beef Commission
North Dakota Wheat Commission
Pace Foods, Ltd.
Perdue® Farms
Reckitt & Colman Inc.
Sargento Foods Inc.®
Southeast United Dairy Industry Association, Inc.
Sunkist Growers, Inc.
Uncle Ben's Rice
Washington Apple Commission
Wisconsin Milk Marketing Board

—Index—

METRIC CONVERSION CHART

VOLUME MEASUREMENTS (dry)

1/8 teaspoon = 0.5 mL
1/4 teaspoon = 1 mL
1/2 teaspoon = 2 mL
3/4 teaspoon = 4 mL
1 teaspoon = 5 mL
1 tablespoon = 15 mL
2 tablespoons = 30 mL
1/4 cup = 60 mL
1/3 cup = 75 mL
1/2 cup = 125 mL
2/3 cup = 150 mL
3/4 cup = 175 mL
1 cup = 250 mL
2 cups = 1 pint = 500 mL
3 cups = 750 mL
4 cups = 1 quart = 1 L

VOLUME MEASUREMENTS (fluid)

1 fluid ounce (2 tablespoons) = 30 mL
4 fluid ounces (1/2 cup) = 125 mL
8 fluid ounces (1 cup) = 250 mL
12 fluid ounces (1 1/2 cups) = 375 mL
16 fluid ounces (2 cups) = 500 mL

WEIGHTS (mass)

1/2 ounce = 15 g
1 ounce = 30 g
3 ounces = 90 g
4 ounces = 120 g
8 ounces = 225 g
10 ounces = 285 g
12 ounces = 360 g
16 ounces = 1 pound = 450 g

DIMENSIONS

1/16 inch = 2 mm
1/8 inch = 3 mm
1/4 inch = 6 mm
1/2 inch = 1.5 cm
3/4 inch = 2 cm
1 inch = 2.5 cm

OVEN TEMPERATURES

250°F = 120°C
275°F = 140°C
300°F = 150°C
325°F = 160°C
350°F = 180°C
375°F = 190°C
400°F = 200°C
425°F = 220°C
450°F = 230°C

BAKING PAN SIZES

Utensil	Size in Inches/Quarts	Metric Volume	Size in Centimeters
Baking or Cake Pan (square or rectangular)	8×8×2	2 L	20×20×5
	9×9×2	2.5 L	22×22×5
	12×8×2	3 L	30×20×5
	13×9×2	3.5 L	33×23×5
Loaf Pan	8×4×3	1.5 L	20×10×7
	9×5×3	2 L	23×13×7
Round Layer Cake Pan	8×1½	1.2 L	20×4
	9×1½	1.5 L	23×4
Pie Plate	8×1¼	750 mL	20×3
	9×1¼	1 L	23×3
Baking Dish or Casserole	1 quart	1 L	—
	1½ quart	1.5 L	—
	2 quart	2 L	—